METHODOLOGY OF TEACHING COMPUTER SCIENCE

DR. P.C. NAGA SUBRAMANI

(M.Sc.,M.Ed.,M.Phil.,Ph.D.)

Department of Education (DDE)
Assistant Professor
Annamalai University
Annamalai Nagar, Chidambaram, Tamil Nadu

Publish World

2014

Price : Rs. 595

First Edition : 2014

ISBN : 978-81-928910-0-2

ISBN Allotment Agency : Raja Rammohun Roy National Agency for ISBN

Published & Printed by

Publish World
10, Toran Bunglows, Near Nandbhumi,
A. V. Road, Anand – 388001
Gujarat (India)
http://www.publishworld.org
Email : pwisbn@gmail.com

PREFACE

This book "METHODOLOGY OF TEACHING COMPUTER SCIENCE" is prepared in accordance with the prescribed syllabi of the B. Ed Degree course of the various universities of Tamilnadu. Although plenty of books in computer education are available in the market, no book has so far been written meeting the latest requirements of the revised curriculum of teacher training programs. By virtue of its extensive and in-depth coverage, this book will help the reader's digest ideas and concepts of the subject across the curriculum and as such it will be highly useful to the students preparing for B. Ed examinations.

This venture is the natural result of an attempt to fill up the gap in the realm of computer education which has been found to be widening with the passage of time in consonance with the rapid expansion of knowledge and consequent innovations in the development and transmission of the school curriculum for science. We have tried to discuss all related concepts of the subject in order to make this attempt effective enough to cater to all relevant issues raised by these enormous changes.

This book is specifically geared to the needs of teacher educators and teacher trainees and it is earnestly hoped that the book will be whole heartedly received by the teacher educators and teacher trainees alike. With immense pleasure we would like to present this inspirational and authoritative book to stimulate and guide teacher educators and teacher trainees. We do not claim perfection in the book. Constructive criticism and suggestions for the improvement and modification of this book before the next edition will be accepted with sincere thanks.

Chidambaram   Dr. P.C. Nagasubramani
24-11-2014

CONTENTS

UNIT – I : AN INTRODUCTION TO TEACHING OF COMPUTER SCIENCE 1 – 14

Introduction – Development of Computer Science as a separate discipline – The necessity of Computer Science teachers - Computer Science become a full discipline - Computer Science becomes a tool for studies in other disciplines – Present status of Computer Science in school curriculum – Teaching of Computer Science in broader perspectives - Computer Science and Information technology – ICT – scope of Computer Science in modern context – Need and importance of Teaching Computer Science – Aims of teaching of Computer Science in schools as separate subject – Objectives of Teaching Computer Science in B.Ed. curriculum – Values of learning Computer Science – A challenge in the Computer Science curriculum.

UNIT – II : OBJECTIVE BASED INSTRUCTION AND ALLIED CONCEPTS 15 – 40

Types of objectives – The changing concept of Educational objectives into instructional objectives – Meaning and significance of instructional objectives – Criteria for selection of objectives – Objectives of Teaching Computer Science – Bloom's taxonomy of Educational objectives – Usefulness of taxonomical classifications – Major objectives and specifications of Computer Science Education – Writing objectives in behavioral terms – Robert Mager's approach for writing instructional objectives – Development of scientific attitude as an objective of Teaching Computer Science – Outcome based teaching and learning in Computer Science Education – Tips to give your lesson in a great way.

UNIT – III : PRINCIPLES AND MAXIMS OF EFFECTIVE TEACHING 41 – 50

General Principles of successful teaching – Maxims of Teaching – Principles of Computer Science curriculum designing – Qualities of Exemplary Computer Science Teachers – Implementation Requirements of Computer Science Curriculum.

UNIT – IV: PLANNING AND PREPARING FOR INSTRUCTION 51 – 80

The benefits of Planning – Developing plans – Approaches to Planning – The concept of Planning for balance – Types of Planning – Year plan – Unit plan – Lesson plan – Lesson plan phases – An ideal lesson plan – Introspection in lesson plan – Models of lesson plan – Format of lesson plan – Lesson plan model.

UNIT – V: COMPUTER SOFTWARE 81 – 90

Meanings of Computer Software – Types of Computer Software – Functions of Computer Software – Procedure for acquiring software – Software ethics – Cyber Computer crime – Cyber laws in India.

UNIT – VI : COMPUTER IN EDUCATION 91 – 122

Roots and rudiments of Educational Computing – Computer in Teaching – Computer in Learning – Computer in Assessment – Computer in Guidance and Counseling – Computer in Distance Learning – Computer in Higher Education – Computer in Special Education – Computer in Educational Research – Computer in Educational Administration – Social Networking as an Educational tool – Computer as Non-Print and print media of Education.

CONTENTS

UNIT – VII : INSTRUCTIONAL METHODS   123 – 129

Programmed Instruction – Personalized system of Instruction (PSI) – Computer Assisted Instruction (CAI) – Teaching Methods.

UNIT – VIII : INSTRUCTIONAL AIDS   130 – 142

Edgar dale's cone of Experience – Projected Aids – Non-Projected Aids – Graphic Aids – Audio Aids – Display Boards – Dimensional Aids – Activity Aids.

UNIT – IX : EVALUATION IN COMPUTER SCIENCE   143 – 165

Uses of Test and Examinations – Objective based teaching and evaluation – Concept of evaluation – Tools and techniques in evaluation – Test and examinations – Different types of test based on purpose – Techniques of evaluation – Criteria of good test – Different types of test – Construction and organization – Computer aided evaluation – On-line examination.

UNIT – X : COMPUTER TECHNOLOGY   166 – 185

The growing capability of computer technology – Robotics – Parts of Robots – Systems in Robots – Uses of Robots – Characteristics of a Robot – Classifications of robots – History of Robots – Kinds of jobs done by Robots – Artificial Intelligence – Approaches to Artificial Intelligence – ICT Intelligence – Computers in office automation – Office automation technologies – Office automation systems.

BIBLIOGRPHY

UNIT – I

AN INTRODUCTION TO TEACHING OF COMPUTER SCIENCE

Introduction

Nowadays, we cannot imagine our life without computers and the fact is that they have become so important that nothing can replace them. They seem to be everywhere today. Since 1948 when the first real computer has been invented our life has changed so much that we call this age as the age of real digital revolution, the world as 'global village' and the modern generation as 'digital natives'. There isn't a place where there isn't a computer involved. Computers are now a necessity in business, homes, schools and every domain of human work. It is an ideal tool for learning, teaching, working, organizing, and even communicating. Without computers, our society, commerce, and economy will not be advancing at the speed that it is now. Today, when the whole world has metamorphosed into a global village wired together through the magical phenomenon of computers, saying that computers have become an indispensable part of our lives, would be a gross understatement. Computers have permeated every aspect of our lives and have indisputably become a necessity in these modern times, without which life today is simply unimaginable.

Computers have revolutionized the world of communication with the introduction of the internet. Information on any topic is just a click away now, leading to increased awareness and a more informed society. Tools such as e-mail and instant messaging have become the standard norms in business communications. Just how important it is to be well versed with computers can be gauged from the fact that this is a pre-requisite for any job opportunity these days. People who have not learned how to navigate through internet and have no basic computer skills will increasingly have a difficult time securing employment. It has been proved to be a powerful educational tool and has modernized teaching methodology around the world. It has also won its way into the hearts of the people as a popular source of entertainment.

Every child in every classroom, every teacher in every school, and every person in every community is influenced by technology and the roots of technology are based on the fundamentals of computer science. We believe that a fundamental understanding of computer science enables students to be not only educated users of technology but also presents them with the possibility of designing and building our future technology tools. Computer science education is strongly based upon the higher tiers of Bloom cognitive taxonomy as it involves design, creativity, problem solving, analyzing a variety of possible solutions to a problem, collaboration, and presentation skills. These skills allow students to express their ideas in ways that will prepare them to face the competitive world and provide them with the knowledge to use computers to improve the quality of life.

1

Development of Computer Science as a separate discipline

For a long time in our schools we have been teaching science in an integrated way through the subject 'General Science', instead of teaching it in the form of separate branches like physics, chemistry, zoology, biology etc. Later this integrated approach became target of criticism with the changing circumstances of the world and the tremendous increase in the knowledge of science, the impact of which was felt in every sphere of our life. So it was conceived that this integrated approach cannot prepare the students for keeping pace with the latest developments in the field of science and technology. So we were forced to change our approach of teaching science in our schools and consequently the integrated approach has been replaced with disciplinary approach in the form of separate specialized branches like physics, chemistry, biology etc instead of teaching science in the form of a mere combination of some fragmented pieces of knowledge in the name of "General Science". With the adoption of 10+2 system, the disciplinary approach gained momentum and different branches of science for this purpose have been segregated into two groups, Computer Science and Life Sciences. This necessitated the need for separate staff for teaching computer science.

The Necessity of Computer Science Teachers

The grouping of science subjects into two distinct groups and the adoption of disciplinary approach with regard to Computer Science teaching have thus necessitated to bring essential changes in the ways and means of training teachers in our universities and training colleges. Instead of training them to teach science subjects, we have started to train them to teach Computer Sciences and life sciences separately to enable them with more sound pedagogical and methodological proficiencies and in-depth knowledge and understanding of the subject. In all the courses irrespective of the discipline teacher trainees are forced to take computer science as a compulsory paper due to its efficiency in giving learning experiences in all disciplines. It is this background, universities of our country have started to make provisions for teaching subject entitled as "teaching of Computer Science".

Computer Science becomes a full discipline

Education enhances pupils' lives as well as their life skills. It prepares young people for a world involving technologies that have not yet been invented, and presents them with technical and ethical challenges of which we are not yet aware. To do this, education aspires primarily to teach disciplines with long-term value, rather than skills with short-term usefulness, although the later are certainly useful. A "discipline" is characterised by:

- **A body of knowledge**, including widely-applicable ideas and concepts, and a theoretical framework into which these ideas and concepts fit.

- **A set of techniques and methods** that may be applied in the solution of problems, and in the advancement of knowledge.
- **A way of thinking and working** that provides a perspective on the world that is distinct from other disciplines.
- **Longevity**: a discipline does not "date" quickly, although the subject advances.
- **Independence from specific technologies,** especially those that have a short shelf-life.

Computer Science is a discipline with all of these characteristics. It encompasses foundational principles (such as the theory of computation) and widely applicable ideas and concepts (such as the use of relational models to capture structure in data). It incorporates techniques and methods for solving problems and advancing knowledge (such as abstraction and logical reasoning), and a distinct way of thinking and working that sets it apart from other disciplines (computational thinking). It has longevity (most of the ideas and concepts that were formulated 20 or more years ago are still applicable today), and every core principle can be taught or illustrated without relying on the use of a specific technology.

Computer Science becomes a tool for studies in other disciplines

In many countries there has been considerable confusion between teaching computer science using a real-world approach and simply using the tools of computer science to support education in other disciplines. Today there is a large body of research evidence supporting use of computer science principles and problem-solving methods to solve "realistic" problems in various domains. Students need to acquire a scientific-engineering interdisciplinary approach to solve complex problems in various domains; hence, computer science should not be taught isolated from mathematics and other sciences. Students should use the tools of computer science to develop knowledge-based projects related to descriptive topics of a qualitative nature. While these calls for an interdisciplinary approach, they should not be construed as an argument for eliminating computer science as a distinct subject of academic study.

Present status of Computer Science in school curriculum

Study of Computer Sciences has been given due place in our school educational programme by being made as a compulsory subject to all pupils as a part of general education during the first ten years of schooling because of its uses, applications and advantages in all aspects of human life. Utility of a subject in one's personal and social life is enough to justify its place in school curriculum. Therefore, the decision of providing a compulsory status for the study of Computer Science is quite justified and valid.

Teaching of Computer Science in broader perspectives

Teaching of Computer Sciences is intended to prepare the students for the 21 century. The broader perspectives that accelerated the teaching of computer science in our schools can be discussed under the following heads.

1. Impact on Modern Communities

Development and progress in the field of Computer Sciences has influenced the life and living of modern communities and societies in so many ways as follows.

    a. Construction of buildings and residential colonies
    b. Transportation and communication systems
    c. Modernization of systems of food production and its availability to the people
    d. Water source management and its purification
    e. Modern means for the entertainment and leisure time hobbies
    f. Health care and treatment of diseases
    g. Development of inter-relationship and dependence

2. Automation

Automation is the use of machines, control systems and information technologies to optimize productivity in the production of goods and delivery of services. The correct incentive for applying automation is to increase productivity, and or quality beyond that which is possible with current human labour levels so as to realize economies of large scale, and or realize predictable quality levels. Now the human life just follows the routine direction that is any job where information can be digitized and key tasks can be broken down into a set of predictable rules. For example, for airline reservations, tickets, boarding passes, one can complete the whole process on the telephone, recognizing simple sentences in response to prompts, then providing the appropriate information without even talking to a human being. So the aim of teaching computer sciences is to prepare the learners for the automated life style of men in all spheres of his life.

Automation has big consequences for education as well. Computers can follow directions better, faster, and cheaper than human labour, and the number of tasks computers can do grows every year._Any curriculum that emphasizes following directions to find a single correct answer is, by definition, preparing students for jobs that probably will not exist by the time those students graduate.

3. Globalization

The term globalization was coined in the 1980's to encapsulate the occurrence of developing interconnectedness of world's population. This interconnectedness has led to an increased interest in globalization. Globalization is not a recently developed concept. However, the rapidly increasing access to the Internet has broadened its reach and intensified its pace. The first version of globalization started when Christopher Columbus discovered that the world was round. The second version of globalization began during the industrial revolution, and the final version started in early 2000. The final version of globalization coupled with computer-mediated communication established a concrete communication network devoted to advancing social connectedness, accessing academic information, and dominating the business world. Computer Science accelerated the process of globalization to a great extent. Suddenly people from different places could collaborate with each other on different kinds of work and share different kinds of knowledge than ever before. Highly skilled people with roughly the same qualifications are competing directly with each other, no matter where they are located on the globe.

Now we can see the evolution of computer science programs toward globalized technological education. It altered the traditional objectives of education into pace learning, self learning, collaborative learning, interactive education, synthesis of knowledge, and objective based education.

4. Work place change

For the past generation, technological inventions and improvements seem to be introduced every week. The trend is guaranteed to continue. So every effort must be made in the schools to ensure that students are prepared for a scientific workplace. The major shifts in the workplace are:

1. Companies focusing more on providing information than "things."
2. Companies are "flatter," with less hierarchy and less direct supervision.
3. Employees have more autonomy and responsibility.
4. Work is much more collaborative.
5. Jobs are less routine, unpredictable, and unstable.
6. Growth of the information-service economy
7. Work has become more challenging and more satisfying

5. Demographic change

Now in an internationalized age, schools should be able to educate a more diverse student population and to prepare students to interact in a more diverse society and collaborate in a more diverse work environment. Demographic shifts are creating a communications gap between teachers, principals, and the students and families they serve, forcing educators to rethink their school communication strategies.

6. Personal risk and responsibility

Individuals now shoulder more responsibility for personal well-being. Job security and employment are more contingent on performance than loyalty. Employment is less secure to those who cannot perform. Retirement coverage is shifting toward individually controlled investments. Occupations requiring more education are predicted to grow faster. Nearly two-thirds of new jobs will require computer education or training. Income inequality has increased massively driven by demand for high-skilled workers. Trades are becoming more technical, requiring stronger computing and problem solving.

Computer Science and Information Technology

Computer Science and Information Technology are complementary subjects. Computer Science teaches a pupil how to be an effective author of computational tools (i.e. software), while IT teaches how to be a thoughtful user of those tools. This neat juxtaposition is only part of the truth, because it focuses too narrowly on computers as a technology, and computing is much broader than that.

- **Computer Science** is a discipline that seeks to understand and explore the world around us, both natural and artificial, in computational terms. Computer Science is particularly, but by no means exclusively, concerned with the study, design, and implementation of computer systems, and understanding the principles underlying these designs.

- **Information Technology** deals with the purposeful application of computer systems to solve real-world problems, including issues such as the identification of business needs, the specification and installation of hardware and software, and the evaluation of usability. It is the productive, creative and explorative use of technology.

We want our children to understand and play an active role in the digital world that surrounds them, not to be passive consumers of an opaque and mysterious technology. A sound understanding of computing concepts will help them to get the best from the systems they use, and to solve problems when things go wrong. Moreover, citizens able to think in computational terms would be able to understand and rationally argue about issues involving computation, such as software patents, identity theft, genetic engineering, electronic voting systems for elections, and so on. In a world suffused by computation, every school-leaver should have an understanding of computing.

ICT

ICT Stands for "Information and Communication Technologies." ICT refers to technologies that provide access to information through telecommunications. It is similar to Information Technology (IT), but focuses primarily on communication technologies. This includes the Internet, wireless networks, cell phones, and other communication mediums. In the past few decades, information and communication technologies have provided society with a vast array of new communication capabilities. For example, people can communicate in real-time with others in different countries using technologies such as instant messaging, voice over IP (VoIP), and video-conferencing. Social networking websites like Face book allow users from all over the world to remain in contact and communicate on a regular basis. Modern information and communication technologies have created a "global village," in which people can communicate with others across the world as if they were living next door. For this reason, ICT is often studied in the context of how modern communication technologies affect society.

The following are the difference between ICT and Computer Science

The study of computer systems and how they are used	The study of how computer systems are built and work
Human need is central to the subject	Computation is central to the subject
Concerned with the design, development and evaluation of systems, with particular emphasis on the data, functional and usability requirements of end users	Concerned with algorithmic thinking, and the ways in which a real-world problem can be decomposed in order to construct a working solution
Focuses on building or programming a solution by using a combination of currently available devices and software.	Solves problems and develops new systems by writing new software and developing innovative computational approaches.
Emphasis on selecting, evaluating, designing and configuring appropriate software and devices. Programming is one method of creating desired outcomes.	Emphasis on principles and techniques for building new software and designing new hardware. Programming and coding is a central technique to create outcomes.
ICT supports, enhances and empowers human activity and informs future developments.	Computation is a "lens" through which we can understand the natural world, and the nature of thought itself, in a new way.
Tending towards the higher level study and application of ICT in a range of contexts, from academic to vocational.	Tending towards higher level academic study of Computing and Computer Science.

Scope of Computer Science in modern context

The scope of any subject can usually be discussed under two heads:

1. The limits of its operations and applications.
2. The branches, topics and the subject matter it deals with.

The field of operation and applications of Computer Science are too wide. The truest areas in Computer Sciences at the present juncture may be named as below.

1. Alternative sources of energy
2. Water sources management
3. Super conductivity, super fluidity, and low temperature phenomena
4. Plasma physical and plasma diagnostic teaching
5. Holography and optical information processing
6. Applied optics
7. Fusion reactors
8. Thermal nuclear energy production
9. The fibre optics information technology
10. Laser engineering

It is very difficult to define the topics and the subject matter in computer science because of the unpredictable changes that happens in information technology.

Need and Importance of Teaching Computer science

Computer Science is the study of principles and practices that underpin an understanding and modelling of computation, and of their application in the development of computer systems. At its heart lies the notion of computational thinking: a mode of thought that goes well beyond software and hardware, and that provides a frame work to reason about systems and problems. This mode of thinking is supported and complemented by a substantial body of theoretical and practical knowledge, and by a set of powerful techniques for analysing, modelling and solving problems.

Computer Science is deeply concerned with how computers and computer systems work, and how they are designed and programmed. Pupils studying computing gain insight into computational systems of all kinds, whether or not they include computers. Computational thinking influences fields such as Biology, Chemistry, Linguistics, Psychology, Economics and Statistics. It allows us to solve problems, design systems and understand the power and limits of human and machine intelligence. It is a skill that empowers, and that all pupils should be aware of and have some competence in. Furthermore, pupils who can think computationally are better able to conceptualise and understand computer-based technology, and so are better equipped to function in modern society.

Computer Science is a practical subject, where invention and resourcefulness are encouraged. Pupils are expected to apply the academic principles they have learned to the understanding of real-world systems, and to the creation of purposeful artefacts. This combination of principles, practice, and invention makes it an extraordinarily useful and an intensely creative subject, suffused with excitement, both visceral ("it works!") and intellectual ("that is so beautiful").

Aims of teaching of Computer Science in schools as a separate subject

The advantages that can be drawn or purposes that can be served by the study of any subject generally become the aim for its study. The following are the aims of teaching of computer science in schools.

1. **Utilitarian aims:** To enable the students to make use of the computer sciences in their day-to-day activities.

2. **Intellectual or mental development aim:** To develop the intellectual or mental abilities of the students that is needed for their academic life and practical life.

3. **Disciplinary aim:** To help the students in making them disciplined in all respects.

4. **Cultural aim:** To help the students in the process of preservation, promotion, and transmission of culture

5. **Moral aim:** To help the students in the development of moral values avoiding false notions and beliefs.

6. **Aesthetic aim:** To help the students in the inculcation of aesthetic sense and artistic values.

7. **Vocational aim:** To help the students in preparing them for the future professions or occupations.

8. **Inter disciplinary aim:** To help the students in utilizing study of computer sciences for the study of other subjects.

9. **Problem solving aim:** To help the students to acquire problem solving ability by training them in scientific method.

10. **Social aim:** To help the students in the process of the development of the society and inculcate social virtues and ideals among the students and prepare them for the 21st century.

Objectives of Teaching Computer Science in B. Ed Curriculum

1. The student teachers acquire knowledge about the aim, need, and importance of teaching computer science at Higher Secondary level.
2. The student teachers understand the need and importance of computer teaching in the school level.
3. The student teachers develop skills to practice operating computer in the class room situation.
4. The student teachers apply the knowledge in the actual class room situations in teaching computer science.
5. The student teachers develop interest to know the recent trends and developments of the computing.

Values of learning Computer Science

Values are the guiding principles governing the lifestyle of the members of a society, which are conducive to all round development of the individuals. Values give meaning and strength to a person's life by occupying a central place in his dealings. Values reflect one's personal attitudes, judgements, decisions, behaviour, relationships, dreams and vision. Values are considered as the navigating stars that provide proper direction to persons. It is because of these facts that our educational system is designed in such a way as to create a value system in man and every subject in the curriculum has its own value system that make a student a better citizen coping with the present status of the world. Computer Science is no exception to this rule. It equips and armours the learner with such a knowledge which will help him to become a useful and efficient citizen of the society. The most important values of learning computer science are as follows:

1. Utilitarian or practical value

Science has revolutioned_our way of living and our lives depend entirely on scientifically invented gadgets so much that we cannot do without them. It is now imperative for everyone not only to understand but also to master it. The knowledge of computer is needed at every stage of life now. It is difficult for a common man to lead a comfortable life without the use of computer knowledge and skills. Computer and technology literacy is a must even for an illiterate for a smooth living adjusting with the changing needs of the society. That is why the study of computer is considered compulsory to all the learners up to a particular level that will lead to possess men with art of economic living, development of will power, attitude towards the spirit of discovery and the power of expression.

2. Disciplinary Value

The study of computer science inculcates the spirit of enquiry, seriousness and systematic thinking and it brings about total transformation of one's viewpoint and makes thinking process more organized, exact, logical and real. It makes us think seriously and helps to observe the real nature of the problem. It helps us to judge all the good and bad points together, with the gain and loss likely to be incurred in the plan of action contemplated. Computer sciences also check one to take a hasty action prompted by one's sentiments and influenced by the biased opinions of others, which are against the principles of science. Study of computer sciences inculcate the habit of viewing a problem impartially with an alert mind and promote interest in study, concentration on habit of hard and systematic work. This helps to lead one's daily life successfully in a well-organized and systematic way. Thus the study of computer sciences develops our personality as a whole.

3. Intellectual Value

Science gives us the insight, which enables us to search the truth and the reality of nature around it. We are able to do useful except anything which we cannot prove by actual observation, reasoning and experimentation. The queries like 'why' and 'how' of all problems and phenomena can be satisfactorily answered only by the wisdom of science. The study of computer science provides the learners the opportunity of developing mental faculties of reasoning, imagination, memory, observation, concentration, analysis, originality and of systematic thinking.

4. Cultural Value

From time immemorial men have been trying to maintain and preserve their way of life and standard through the use of science. But our way of life has been changing with the passage of time and progress of science. We can say that the development of culture is the history of science and we can judge the progress of the nation by its progress in science. We are constantly adjusting and modifying our style of living according to the greatest invention and discoveries. Therefore, the study of computer science not only develops the culture of a society and nation but also helps in preserving it and one of the aims of education to impart cultural values among the individuals is achieved.

5. Vocational Value

A sound and productive vocational life demands a sound computer background because it finds extensive application in all vocations and its minute areas. Each and every person needs computer knowledge for earning and to maintain his living standard. Now we can safely claim that the study of computer sciences have a great "bread and butter value" preparing the citizens for earning their livelihood in their future life.

6. Moral Value

The qualities of honesty of purpose, truth, justice, punctuality, determination, patience, self-control, self-respect, self-confidence and tolerance are automatically developed of one follows scientific method in pursuit of knowledge. The person busy in pursuit of truth and reality imbibes in himself the qualities of morality. The desirable trait of character developed through the study of computer science are the habit of lawfulness, the faculty of distinction between right and wrong and the respect for other's point of view. In computer sciences every conclusion depends upon tests and actual observations and not by cheat and deceit.

7. Aesthetic Value

Science is a beauty, art, a source of entertainment and an effective means of attaining physical comforts. The study of science is a source of great pleasure when one gets answers to his queries about the mysteries of nature. Study of computer science help us to utilize our leisure purposefully providing scientific gadgets for our entertainment like cinema, drawing, newspapers, scientific hobbies etc. Thus computer science plays a considerable role in the development of various arts.

8. Social Value

What we do in our present society totally depends upon the progress and development brought out by the study of Computer Sciences. It has given eyes to the society in the form of microscopes, cameras, i-pads, laptops and supersonic jets. The globalization and proximity brought out by the progress in the Computer Sciences has necessitated developing social, democratic and humanistic values in the individuals for the welfare and their own adjustment in the society. Study of Computer Sciences provides great impetus and opportunities for the development and progress of the society, useful experiences of the society and inculcation of social values and virtues in the students.

9. Problem solving ability training

Students of computer sciences get enough opportunities for being trained in the use of scientific method and scientific approach for the solution of the problems. In general the following thought process is involved in solving a problem through scientific method in Computer Sciences.

1. The nature and purpose of the problem.
2. Analysis of the problem.
3. Testing the validity of the various solutions of the problem.
4. Testing the results through applications in other problems of similar nature.

10. Self sufficiency of learning till graveyard

Teaching computer means giving learners a gift for the future that gives them the lifelong learning skills. In future, learners need not be tied to particular locations. They will be able to study at home, at work, or in a local library or shopping centre, as well as in colleges and universities. People will be able to study at a distance using broadcast media and on-line access. Our aim should be to help students to learn wherever they choose and whatever they choose and support them in assessing how they are doing and where they want to go next. Exploring the use of lifelong learner records linked to foundation degrees, work-based learning, open linking between schools, colleges, learning providers, higher education institutions, etc., distributed e-learning focuses on the learner, rather than the institution. So it is the **shared** responsibility of the school, homes, and the society to make the young equipped with latest tools for their smooth survival in the modern age.

A Challenge in the Computer Science Curriculum

One of the challenges we face when discussing computer science education is that the field of computer science seems to evolve so quickly that it is difficult to clearly define its contents and prescribe its boundaries. Computer science is neither programming nor computer literacy. Rather, it is "the study of computers and algorithmic processes including their principles, their hardware and software design, their applications, and their impact on society" Computer science therefore includes: programming, hardware design, networks, graphics, databases and information retrieval, computer security, software design, programming languages, logic, programming paradigms, translation between levels of abstraction, artificial intelligence, the limits of computations, applications in information technology and information systems, and social issues (Internet security, privacy, intellectual property, etc.). Computer Science, in contrast to Information Technology or Educational Technology, spans a wide range of computing endeavours, from theoretical foundations to robotics, computer vision, intelligent systems, and bioinformatics.

Computer Science is the baby in the world of school subjects. Maths, Science, History, Geography, Literature and Languages have been taught in schools since the days of Plato. The teaching of these subjects is rooted in hundreds of years of experience and has arguably not changed a great deal in our lifetime. Computer Science has only been taught in schools since the eighties and our subject matter is constantly changing and evolving. So we cannot design a curriculum even for five years because of the unpredictable changes in the field of information technology. So there must be constant and continuous mentoring, revising, and changing of curriculum along with the teacher training programs, faculty development programs and in-service programs.

UNIT – II

OBJECTIVE BASED INSTRUCTION AND ALLIED CONCEPTS

Every day, teachers make a wide variety of instructional decisions that directly affect the students' learning. These decisions ranges from the choice of materials, pacing and sequencing of activities, the ways of reinforcing pupil's learning and means of assessing whatever the students have learnt. Different types of learning require different learning experiences and hence different types of objectives.

Types of Objectives

1. Behavioural objectives

Behavioural objectives describe what the learner will be able to do after completing the learning event. This type of objective is valued for its directness and clarity. A well-written set of behavioural objectives can truly:

- Define the scope of the training.
- Set the learner's expectation of what he/she can expect to get out of the training.
- Guide the designer through establishing the instructional and evaluation approaches.
- Establish certification criteria.

2. Experiential objectives

Experiential objectives are used to elicit a predetermined attitude or behaviour through a carefully selected set of learning experiences. The learning environment is actually engineered to bring about the desired change in attitude and/or behaviour. This approach is commonly used to affect values and beliefs. Experiential training often leads to follow-up activities, including changes to lifestyle.

3. Expressive objectives

Expressive objectives are used to provide the learner with an engineered opportunity for personal discovery and/or enlightenment. In contrast to experiential training, expressive training does not attempt to yield a predetermined effect. The learning is entirely dependent on the self-discovery. This approach is commonly used to expose learners to new experiences and to discover new interests or unknown talent.

15

The changing concept of Educational Objectives into Instructional Objectives

We may broadly define educational objective as purposes and aims. However, they are often defined in terms of outcomes of different kinds, classes, categories and levels. An educational objective is said to be 'the product of value judgement' which in practice presents a decision taken by some persons as a worthy end.

The judgment should be the best possible one under the circumstances. In order that the decision is sound it could be in the fitness of things to proceed towards it in a systematic manner. This involves work of three kinds:

a) derivation and statement of objectives;
b) classification of objectives;
c) definition of objectives in terms of behavioural outcomes for actual classroom practices.

Broadly speaking, the first category of work is of a general rather than of an abstract nature. This yields major ideas for developing objectives, which on being translated into specific statements, helps in developing an instructional program and in specifying the types of courses required at different levels.

The second category of such effort is needed for further classification and understanding of these objectives by discovering a system among them and articulating them appropriately in terms of an educational programme.

Finally, there is the category of action which pertains to the definition of objectives at an operational level for a particular curricular area. This calls for the statements of learning situations, the nature of behaviour expected and the extent of achievement or behaviour modification visualized. Teaching-learning situation, activities, and evaluation programmes directly flow from there. These are termed as instructional objectives.

Meaning and Significance of Instructional Objectives

In order to align instruction in the classroom, teachers must be goal-oriented during the planning and execution of lessons. This means instruction should be objective-based. Objective-based instruction requires teachers to set learning goals and objectives prior to instruction. After the learning objective has been clearly established and stated in measurable, behavioral terms, the teacher then selects those activities and learning experiences that are congruent to and support the intended objective. An instructional objective describes the specific teaching outcome; the behaviour required to perform it and determines the means for measuring or evaluating it. Such evaluation is based on the directional statements that identify the expected learner outcomes, establish purposes and stipulate levels of achievement. Instructional objectives are specific and arc behavioural in nature. These are mainly based on specific observable or measurable goals in pupil's learning. An instructional objective establishes a minimal level of attainment for deciding whether or not the desired learning has been achieved.

An instructional objective may describe the mediating conditions under which the behaviour is to be achieved, as well as provides the procedures for determining whether or not a certain level of attainment has occurred. Instructional objectives state both what behaviour is intended to be developed (curricular aspect) and what actual behavioural is developed and tested (evaluation aspect). Instructional objectives are thus nothing but descriptions of pupils' terminal behaviour expected out of the ongoing classroom instruction. So at the time of imparting instructions that is teaching of a particular lesson unit or sub-units of the object computer science, a teacher has to place before him some definite and very specific objectives to be attained within a specified classroom period and resources in hand.

Criteria for Selection of Objectives

1. In tune with aims of education
2. Utility of the subject and usefulness for the students
3. Specific in terms of means, ends and time frame
4. Feasibility of application
5. Consideration of the nature of the learner, the subject, and the society
6. Psychology of learning and instruction
7. Philosophy of education and the present status of the learner
8. Socio economic condition of contemporary society

Objectives of teaching Computer Sciences

1. Development of process like observation, classification, communication, measurement, estimation, prediction etc.
2. Acquisition and understanding of knowledge, development of the skills for problem solving and investigation, ability to think logically as well as to draw conclusion on the basis of experiments.
3. Development of the ability to reach generalizations and to apply them for solving life problems.
4. Development of understanding of inter-relationship of computer science and society.
5. Fostering of creativity leading to innovation in computer science.
6. Preparing the young generation for the new world of technology.

Bloom's Taxonomy of Educational Objectives

One of the most widely used ways of organizing levels of expertise is according to Bloom's Taxonomy of Educational Objectives. Bloom's Taxonomy uses a multi-tiered scale to express the level of expertise required to achieve each measurable student outcome. Organizing measurable student outcomes in this way will allow us to select appropriate classroom assessment techniques for the course. There are three taxonomies. The taxonomy related to the Cognitive Domain, Affective Domain and Psychomotor Domain.

A. Cognitive Domain Taxonomy of Objectives

The cognitive domain involves knowledge and the development of intellectual skills. This includes the recall or recognition of specific facts, procedural patterns, and concepts that serve in the development of intellectual abilities and skills. There are six major categories, which are listed in order below, starting from the simplest behaviour to the most complex. The categories can be thought of as degrees of difficulties. That is, the first one must normally be mastered before the next one can take place.

1. Knowledge

Knowledge is defined as remembering of previously learned material. This may involve the recall of a wide range of material, from specific facts to complete theories, but all that is required is the bringing of appropriate information to the mind. Knowledge represents the lowest level of learning outcomes in the cognitive domain. Knowledge involves the recall of specifics and universals, the recall of methods and processes, or the recall of a pattern, structure, or setting. For measurement purposes, the recall situation involves little more than bringing to mind the appropriate material may be required, this is relatively minor part of the task. The knowledge objectives emphasize most the psychological processes of remembering.

The knowledge category includes 12 categories. They are as follows:

1. Knowledge of symbols with concrete reference
2. Knowledge of terminology
3. Knowledge of specific facts
4. Knowledge of ways and means of dealing with specifics
5. Knowledge of conventions
6. Knowledge of trends and sequences
7. Knowledge of classifications and categories
8. Knowledge of criteria
9. Knowledge of methodology
10. Knowledge of universals and abstractions in a field
11. Knowledge of principles and generalizations
12. Knowledge of theories and structures

2. Comprehension

Comprehension is defined as the ability to grasp the meaning of material. This represents the lowest level of understanding. It refers to a type of understanding or apprehension such that the individual knows what is being communicated and can make use of the material or seeing its fullest implications. When students are confronted with a communication, they are expected to know what is being communicated (orally or in written form) and be able to make some use of the material or ideas contained in it. This may be shown by:

1. **Translation**: Translating material from one form to another or translating or summarizing the communicated knowledge in his own words.

2. **Interpretation**: By interpreting material we mean cite examples, discriminate, classify and verify.

3. **Exploration**: By exploration we mean, estimating or understanding future trends (predicting consequences or effects) by the use of knowledge and extend it to other subjects and fields.

These learning outcomes go one step beyond the simple remembering of material, and represent the lowest level of understanding. On the ladder of acquisition of cognitive abilities its level is little higher than the knowledge.

3. Application

Application refers to the ability to use learned material in new and concrete situations. This may include the application of such things as rules, methods, concepts, principles, laws, and theories. Learning outcomes in this area require a higher level of understanding than those under comprehension. The distinction between Comprehension and Application is that, the student must know the abstraction well enough that he can correctly demonstrate its use when asked to do so. Application, however, requires a step beyond this. Given a problem, the student must apply the having to be shown how to use it in that situation. Comprehension shows that the student can use it correctly. Application shows he will use it correctly. Under this objective the learner is required to acquire the ability to make use of the abstract or generalized ideas, principles in the particular and concrete situations.

Information and skills become useful when they can be applied to a new, not previously encountered situation. Generalizations can be used to solve new problems. Previous experience can be used to predict outcomes, estimate answers, extrapolate from data, and/or avoid errors. It is important that students have experience applying whatever they learn to new problems and situations. At the application level most of the time we are looking for convergent thinking.

4. Analysis

Analysis refers to the ability to break down material into its component parts so that its organizational structure may be understood. This may include the identification of the parts, analysis of the relationships between parts, and recognition of the organizational principles involved. Learning outcomes here represent a higher intellectual level than comprehension and application because they require an understanding of both the content and the structural form of the material. The breakdown of a communication into its constituent elements or parts such that the relative hierarchy of ideas is made and or the relations between the ideas expressed are made explicit. Such analyses are intended to clarify the communication, to indicate how the communication is organized, and the way in which it manages to convey its effects, as well as its basis and arrangement.

Creative thinking and problem solving begin with analytic thinking: mentally taking something apart to understand better the relationship of the parts to each other and to the whole. To analyze, one must be able to think categorically: that is to organize and reorganize information into categories. Once students can "take information apart" to better understand interrelationships, they are ready to reorganize that information in new patterns and create with it.

In short Analysis includes:
1. Analysis of elements
2. Analysis of relationships
3. Analysis of organizational relationships

5. Synthesis

Synthesis refers to the ability to put parts together to form a new whole. This may involve the production of a unique communication (theme or speech), a plan of operations (research proposal), or a set of abstract relations (scheme for classifying information). Learning outcomes in this area stress creative behaviours, with major emphasis on the formulation of new patterns or structures.

The fifth category of complexity in thinking is synthesis or invention: the creation of something that is new to its creator. One difference between application and synthesis is that usually the former is convergent but the latter is result from divergent thinking: something new and different. Note, however, that a student can create only after s/he has skill and information which then are applied divergently to a new situation. Creativity does not spring from a vacuum but emerges from rigor and structure. In this way, it calls for the creativity aspect of the cognitive abilities and therefore may be considered definitely a higher level of learning involving knowledge comprehension, application as well as analysis.

In other words, Synthesis includes
1. Production of unique communication
2. Production of a plan or proposed set of operations
3. Derivation of a set of abstract relations

6. Evaluation

Evaluation is concerned with the ability to judge the value of material (statement, novel, poem, research report) for a given purpose. The judgements are to be based on definite criteria. These may be internal criteria (organization) or external criteria (relevance to the purpose) and the student may determine the criteria or be given them. Learning outcomes in this area are highest in the cognitive hierarchy because they contain elements of all the other categories, plus conscious value judgements based on clearly defined criteria.

Evaluation, the making of judgments when there is no one answers which is right for everyone, is one of the most complex levels of thinking because evaluation is based on all other cognitive levels. Evaluation or judgment is essential to all intelligent and satisfying decisions. It is judgments about the value of material and methods for given purposes. Evaluation represents definitely the higher level of objectives belonging to the cognitive domain and involves all the five categories described earlier. As a result the learner is expected to take and arrive in proper decision about the matter and methods by making use of all cognitive abilities through the earlier categories of cognitive objectives.

Levels	Behavioural Descriptions	Examples of activity to be trained	Key Words
1. **Knowledge**	Memorizing information, defining techniques, etc.	Multiple-choice test, recount facts or statistics, recall a process, rules, definitions; quote law or procedure	Arrange, define, describe, label, list, memorise, recognise, relate, reproduce, select, state
2.**Comprehension**	Understand meaning, re-state data in one's own words, interpret, extrapolate, translate	Explain or interpret meaning from a given scenario or statement, suggest treatment, reaction or solution to given problem, create examples or metaphors	Explain, reiterate, reword, critique, classify, summarise, illustrate, translate, review, report, discuss, re-write, estimate, interpret, theorise, paraphrase, reference, example

3. Application	Use or apply knowledge, put theory into practice, use knowledge in response to real circumstances	Put a theory into practical effect, demonstrate, solve a problem, manage an activity	Use, apply, discover, manage, execute, solve, produce, implement, construct, change, prepare, conduct, perform, react, respond, role-play
4. Analysis	Interpret elements, organizational principles, structure, construction, internal relationships; quality, reliability of individual components	Identify constituent parts and functions of a process or concept, or de-construct a methodology or process, making qualitative assessment of elements, relationships, values and effects; measure requirements or needs	Analyse, break down, catalogue, compare, quantify, measure, test, examine, experiment, relate, graph, diagram, plot, extrapolate, value, divide
5. Synthesis	Develop new unique structures, systems, models, approaches, ideas; creative thinking, operations gathering information from several sources	Develop plans or procedures, design solutions, integrate methods, resources, ideas, parts; create teams or new approaches, write protocols or contingencies	Develop, plan, build, create, design, organise, revise, formulate, propose, establish, assemble, integrate, re-arrange, modify
6. Evaluation	Assess effectiveness of whole concepts, in relation to values, outputs, efficacy, viability; critical thinking, strategic comparison and review; judgement relating to external criteria	Review strategic options or plans in terms of efficacy, return on investment or cost-effectiveness, practicability; assess sustainability; perform a SWOT analysis in relation to alternatives; produce a financial justification for a proposition or venture, calculate the effects of a plan or strategy; perform a detailed and costed risk analysis with recommendations and justifications	Review, justify, assess, present a case for, defend, report on, investigate, direct, appraise, argue, project-manage

B. Affective Domain Taxonomy of Objectives

Bloom's theory advocates this structure and sequence for developing attitude - also now commonly expressed in the modern field of personal development as 'beliefs'. Again, as with the other domains, the Affective Domain detail provides a framework for teaching, training, assessing and evaluating the effectiveness of training and lesson design and delivery, and also the retention by and affect upon the learner or trainee. The affective domain includes objectives which describe changes in interest, attitudes and values, and the development of appreciations and adequate adjustment. This domain has a pattern of development similar to the cognitive domain. At the lowest level, the child is merely aware of the fact that other people have particular attitudes and values. As children progress through personal experience, they slowly develop affective ideas which are uniquely their own. Again, it is felt that teaching should be directed towards this end rather than merely indoctrinating the child with the attitudes and values held by the teacher. Although some people would hold that there are some values which must be indoctrinated - respect for others' rights, honesty etc. - there is a school of thought which would seek to have these attitudes and values achieved by the child without this approach, through a process of development and clarification.

The five major categories of Affective Domain are listed from the simplest behaviour to the most complex:

1. Receiving (Attending)
   a. Awareness
   b. Willingness to receive
   c. Controlled or selected attention

This level is defined as one's awareness, willingness to hear, and their selected attention. For the student, teachers will provide instruction that demands their focus and full awareness. The teachers have been trained to switch topics and activities frequently and that no activity outside of assessment is to last beyond 20 minutes. Teachers are becoming open-minded to the learner's position in the classroom. They are to be present and mindful of individual circumstances but present as an alert and focused authority figure. Our hope is that the attitudes demonstrated by the teacher will permeate through the student body present in the classroom. Some of the actions that would be associated with this level might be one's willingness to learn other's names or showing the respect for another's opinion regardless of their personal feelings. To meet the needs of this level the classrooms incorporate several name-learning activities as well as requiring students to write their names any problems they work on the board. Board-work is a great activity for early development and acquisition of computer science related concepts, but that is a whole new Hub. Here the learner is sensitized to the existence of certain phenomena, willing to receive or to attend to them.

2. Responding
   a. Acquiescence in responding
   b. Willingness to respond
   c. Satisfaction in response

This level is defined as the active participation on the part of the learners. The student is present, attentive, and reacts to a particular phenomenon. Some of the behaviours associated with this domain might include the student participating in class discussions, giving a presentation, or questioning new ideals, concepts, models, etc. in order to fully understand them. By providing various levels of assessment the hope is that the student finds success on at least one of the assessment types and that the student can then build off of those efforts. Again, board-work is helpful in building this confidence and addressing this level of the Affective Domain. The more a student's confidence is developed the better this level can be met. Changing the teaching philosophy from a testing-based one to a student-cantered one is foreign to many teachers, but most teachers do care about their student and want them to succeed.

3. Valuing
   a. Acceptance of value
   b. Preference for a value
   c. Commitment

This level is defined as the worth or value a person attaches to a particular object, phenomenon, or behaviour. This can range from simple acceptance to the more complex states of commitment. Valuing is based on the internalization of a set of specified values, while clues to these values are expressed in the learner's outward behaviour and are often recognizable and identifiable. Some of the behaviours associated with this domain are that the learner demonstrates the ability to solve problems or proposes a plan or strategy to solve an application-type problem. This level is being met through homework choices. Students are encouraged to work computer science problems from their text in an effort that the student places value on their efforts. This is addressed in a separate Hub, but this in the domain that exercise tempts to meet. The student is to realize on their own the value of acquiring skill sets and develops individual strategies on how to make connections with the material. The teacher aids in this process by being prepared for class, staying energized and positive about the material, and staying on topic. Returning assignments graded in a prompt manner reminds students that the assessment had value and that their efforts were not in vain.

4. Organizing
   a. Conceptualization of a value
   b. Organization of a value system

This level is defined as the student who organizes values into priorities by contrasting different values, resolving conflicts between them, and creating a unique value system. The emphasis is on comparing, relating, and synthesizing values. Some of the behaviour associated with this level is the ability of the student to recognize the need for balance between freedom and responsible behaviour. The student accepts responsibility for their behaviour and can explain the role of systematic planning in solving problems. The organized student can prioritize time effectively to meet the needs of school, family, and self. Computer science teacher should focus much effort on creating classroom rapport and seek a developed unity by the student that is an evolving for throughout the year. This will help students focus and build a network to stay organized in their studies, and the assessment structure that The Bloom's Taxonomy Project has laid out will allow students the ability to organize their thoughts better. If students are allowed to progress through the cognitive domain naturally, the organization of ideas has a better chance of being successful. Teachers are to help students prepare for assessments appropriately and to direct their emphasis properly both inside the classroom and outside.

5. Characterization
    a. Generalized set
    b. Characterization by a value or value complex

This level is defined as the student who organizes values into priorities by contrasting different values, resolving conflicts between them, and creating a unique value system. The emphasis is on comparing, relating, and synthesizing values. Some of the associated behaviours of the learner might be that the student shows self-reliance when working independently, cooperates in group activities (displays teamwork), uses an objective approach when problem solving, and the student displays a professional commitment to ethical practice on a daily basis. The student also has the ability to revise judgments and changes behaviour in light of new evidence. This level will probably only be met by the student who is achieving at a high level in the classroom. The web-search activity assigned to the students seeks to question their ingrained computational ideas and allows them to develop new thought process beyond what the classroom delivers. If the student is so bold as to assist another individual by sharing their own personal understanding of a subject then student is also meeting their emotional needs of this level as well. At this highest stage of Affective Domain, the learner is destined to imbibe typical characteristics of his individual character that is life style of his own. In fact it is the end point or ultimate goal of the process of education.

Levels	Behavioural Descriptions	Examples of activity to be trained	Key Words
Receiving	open to experience, willing to hear	listen to teacher or trainer, take interest in session or learning experience, take notes, turn up, make time for learning experience, participate passively	ask, listen, focus, attend, take part, discuss, acknowledge, hear, be open to, retain, follow, concentrate, read, do, feel
Responding	react and participate actively	participate actively in group discussion, active participation in activity, interest in outcomes, enthusiasm for action, question and probe ideas, suggest interpretation	react, respond, seek clarification, interpret, clarify, provide other references and examples, contribute, question, present, cite, become animated or excited, help team, write, perform

Valuing	attach values and express personal opinions	decide worth and relevance of ideas, experiences; accept or commit to particular stance or action	argue, challenge, debate, refute, confront, justify, persuade, criticise,
Organising	reconcile internal conflicts; develop value system	qualify and quantify personal views, state personal position and reasons, state beliefs	build, develop, formulate, defend, modify, relate, prioritise, reconcile, contrast, arrange, compare
Characterization	adopt belief system and philosophy	self-reliant; behave consistently with personal value set	act, display, influence, solve, practice,

C. Psychomotor Domain Taxonomy of Objectives

The Psychomotor Domain was ostensibly established to address skills development relating to manual tasks and physical movement, however it also concerns and covers modern day business and social skills such as communications and operation IT equipment, Thus, 'motor' skills extend beyond the originally traditionally imagined manual and physical skills, so always consider using this domain, even if you think your environment is covered adequately by the Cognitive and Affective Domains. Whatever the training situation, it is likely that the Psychomotor Domain is significant. The Dave version of the Psychomotor Domain is featured most prominently here because it is the most relevant and helpful for work- and life-related development, although the Psychomotor Domains suggested by Simpson and Harrow are more relevant and helpful for certain types of adult training and development, as well as the teaching and development of young people and children, so do explore them all. Each has its uses and advantages.

The psychomotor domain includes physical movement, coordination, and use of the motor-skill areas. Development of these skills requires practice and is measured in terms of speed, precision, distance, procedures, or techniques in execution. The 5 major categories are listed from the simplest behaviour to the most complex:

1. Imitation
    a. Impulsion
    b. Overt repetition

It is the lowest level of neuro - muscular activity. It starts as impulse and may grow into an overt act with the capacity to repeat the performance. For the learning of a psychomotor activity, the task begins with the imitation of the observed acts. The child observes the demonstrated behaviour and he feels an inner push or an impulse to imitate action. It is followed by the over repetition of the demonstrated behaviour.

When the student is exposed to an observable action, he begins to make a covert imitation of the action. Imitation begins with inner rehearsal of the muscular system guided by an inner push or an impulse to imitate action. Such covert behaviour appears to be the starting point in the growth of psychomotor skill. This is then followed by overt performance of an act and the capacity to repeat it. The performance however lacks neuromuscular coordination or control, and hence it is generally in a crude form.

2. Manipulation
    a. Following direction
    b. Selection
    c. Fixation

It involves differentiating among various movements and selecting the proper one. This category emphasized manipulation on the part of the learner for the acquisition of skills by following directions, performing selected action and fixation of performance through necessary practice. At this level, the student should be capable of performing an act according to instructions rather than just on basis of observation as is the case at the level of imitation. He begins to differentiate between one set of act from another and is able to select the required act. He begins to attain skill in manipulating chosen elements. With sufficient practice of selected action, he gradually moves towards the fixation of action. At this level the performance is fairly well set. That is to say, the act is performed with relatively greater ease, though with certain amount of consciousness. The response is not automatic at this level.

3. Precision
    a. Reproduction
    b. Control

Here the learner is able to perform skilled acts or motor activities with a desired level of precision and as such the learner may reach a higher level of refinement in reproducing a given act or skilled task. The practice and repetition of performance will decrease the faults in performance. Precision is related with speed, accuracy, proportion, and exactness in performance.

At the level of precision, the proficiency of performance reaches a higher level of refinement in reproducing a given act. The accuracy and exactness in performance become significant. The student does not need a model to reproduce or to guide his action. He is able to increase or decrease the speed of the action and introduce several variations according to specific requirements of different situations. Performance at this stage is accompanied by confidence and also by conscious vigilance.

4. Articulation
    a. Sequence
    b. Harmony

At this stage learner becomes capable of coordinating a series of acts by establishing appropriate sequence and accomplishing harmony or internal consistency among different acts. In other words, the learner will be able to handle many actions in unison and this ability involves coordination in action.

This category of behaviour emphasizes the coordination of a series of acts by establishing an appropriate sequence and accomplishing harmony or internal consistency among different acts. In many practical situations, as you know, not one but several acts are to be performed and different parts of the body are involved. The student becomes able to perform them in a harmonious manner with appropriate articulation in terms of time, speed, and other relevant variables. He develops proficiency in performing a number of related acts simultaneously and sequentially and thereby can produce the desired effect.

5. Naturalization
   a. Automation
   b. Interlamination

It is the highest stage reached in terms of the development or proficiency acquired in the learning of a skill or psychomotor act. Here the learner may reach perfection in performance. On attaining perfection, actions become automatic. In this stage, learner can perform a single act, or series of articulated acts with a greater refinement, ease and convenience as automatic and naturally as possible.

This category refers to naturalization of the single act or a series of articulated acts. At this stage, the skill of performance attains its highest level of proficiency and the act is performed with the least expenditure of psychic energy. The act is routinized to such an extent that it results in an automatic and spontaneous response. Ultimately, it is automatised to the extent that it is carried out unconsciously. The student does not even know that the act is being performed, until he is obstructed or severely disturbed. In other words, the habit of performance becomes his second nature.

Levels	Behavioural Descriptions	Examples of activity to be trained	Key Words
Imitation	copy action of another; observe and replicate	watch teacher or trainer and repeat action, process or activity	copy, follow, replicate, repeat, adhere
Manipulation	reproduce activity from instruction or memory	carry out task from written or verbal instruction	re-create, build, perform, execute, implement
Precision	execute skill reliably, independent of help	perform a task or activity with expertise and to high quality without assistance or instruction; able to demonstrate an activity to other learners	demonstrate, complete, show, perfect, calibrate, control,

Articulation	adapt and integrate expertise to satisfy a non-standard objective	relate and combine associated activities to develop methods to meet varying, novel requirements	construct, solve, combine, coordinate, integrate, adapt, develop, formulate, modify, master
Naturalization	automated, unconscious mastery of activity and related skills at strategic level	define aim, approach and strategy for use of activities to meet strategic need	design, specify, manage, invent, project-manage

Usefulness of Taxonomical Classifications

The usefulness of the taxonomical classification of instructional objectives is often disputed. It, therefore, appears necessary at this place to summarise some of the uses to which it can be put, particularly for testing the students by the student-teachers.

1. Since categories in the Taxonomy are arranged on the principle of graded complexity, the scheme is very useful in identifying the meaningful level at which the learner is working.

2. The techniques and tools of assessment can be relevantly decided upon and developed. Their categorization becomes easy and clear.

3. It will be helpful in translating into practice the principal of comprehensiveness of evaluation by ensuring proper coverage of various aspects of pupils' growth.

4. The examination of the evaluation devices in terms of their validity will be facilitated.

5. The evaluation may prove to be very helpful in arriving at a meaningful synthesis of the various dimensions of a pupil's growth. Identification of areas of interrelationship among the three domains may be of particular significance in this regard.

6. The logical nature of categorisation helps in identifying and grading teaching-learning situations which can be an important source of selecting proper testing situations too.

7. Curriculum development and preparation of instructional material should profit from such a scheme of classification in many ways. Preparation and analysis of textbooks based on well defined objectives may prove to be a big improvement.

8. The classification through its well defined criteria will provide a bridge for further communication among teachers, between teachers and evaluators, curriculum and research workers, psychologists and other behavioural scientists.

9. The taxonomy has also opened new avenues for research in education. Empirical validation of the Taxonomies besides being a worthy area of research in its own way will open new vistas of work.

10. Teachers may be motivated to undertake experimentation on objective based teaching and testing. The scope is likely to become more wide and varied in due course of time.

Major objectives and specifications of Computer Science Education

The three domains are not totally independent of each other, but inter-related. Along with the development of cognitive behavior, there may or may not be changes in the other two domains. So it is not possible to build water-tight compartments separating these three domains. Moreover, in certain aspects, the different objective specified in the taxonomy of a particular domain may overlap. Hence a judicial selection of objectives may become necessary for the practicing computer science teacher. Taking all the studies in the field into consideration, the following instructional objectives and specifications (the observable and measurable behavioral change that occur as a result of realizing an objective is termed as specification or specific objective; and an objective can have more than one specification each of which can be cited as an evidence for the attainment of the objective) to be taken care of at the time of instruction, by a computer teacher.

I. Acquisition of Knowledge (Knowledge level)

Objectives: The learners acquire knowledge of computer terms, facts, conventions, definitions, concepts, principles, properties, phenomena and laws in computer science.

Specifications: The learners

1. Recalls – terms, definitions, principles, properties etc.
2. Recognizes - terms, definitions, principles, properties etc.

Development of Understanding (Understanding level)

Objectives: The learners understand terms, facts, conventions, definitions, concepts, principles, properties, phenomena and laws in computer science.

Understanding of ideas conveyed through different means of communication. The learner is able to interpret and translate ideas.

Specifications: The learners

1. Cite examples
2. Explain the terms and definitions
3. Describe and illustrate phenomena
4. Define concepts
5. Detect errors and give reasons
6. Identify relations
7. Interpret graphs and charts
8. Distinguish and discriminate concepts and give generalizations
9. Compare and classify concepts and find similarities
10. Interpret situations and summarize details
11. Criticize viewpoints and support arguments
12. Locate and rectify errors or gaps
13. See relationship between cause and effects
14. Verify facts, principles, data of computer science

II.   Application of Knowledge (Application level)

Objectives: The learners apply the acquired knowledge and understanding of computer science to unfamiliar situations.

Specifications: The learners

1. Analyze complex situations
2. Give new illustration of principle
3. Verify conclusions, results, etc.
4. Make hypothesis and interpret observation
5. Interpret relations and observations
6. Find reasons for phenomena relations
7. Draw inferences from analyzed data
8. Establish relations and relates principles
9. Predict probable consequences
10. Suggest rectification and alternative methods
11. Arrive generalizations
12. Prepares a systematic and sequential plan for observation and programming
13. Select a language, software, procedure etc.
14. Suggest improvising to software etc.

III. Development of Skill (Skill level)

Objectives: The learners develop practical skills, writing programmes, operating computers, drawing, observation, and labels of computer.

Specifications: The learners

1. Select suitable commands to perform a particular operation
2. Operate the system and allied machines properly
3. Detect errors with speed and accuracy
4. Check the operating systems
5. Represent observation by diagram, graphs, etc.
6. Make simple programmes and finalize the results
7. Explain procedures, processes, conclusions etc.
8. Select the proper operators for calculation
9. Draw figures to given specifications
10. Label the figures appropriately
11. Read commands, charts, or labels

IV. Development of Interest (Interest level)

Objectives: The learners develop interest in the world of computer science in dealing with the various aspects and utilities related to computer sciences.

Specifications: The learners

1. Voluntarily studies literature related to computer science
2. Spends leisure time in various activities related to computer science
3. Closely observe social processes
4. Discuss and readily communicate various aspects of computer science
5. Participate in computer science debates and seminars
6. Improvise simple components
7. Collect components, models etc.
8. Collect information about different aspects of computer science

V. Development of Attitude (Attitude level)

Objectives: The learners develop desirable positive and scientific attitude towards computer science.

Specifications: The learners

1. Show willingness to consider new ideas and shows curiosity to facts and phenomena related to computers.
2. React favorably to the efforts made for use of computers towards human welfare.
3. Describe a scientific phenomenon in clear, concise, and accurate language.
4. Develop intellectual integrity.
5. Use materials economically.
6. Adopt scientific and systematic procedure of work
7. Derive intellectual satisfaction from his pursuit of computer science
8. Show spirit of team work, self-help and self-reliance
9. Respect the teacher of computer science
10. Keep the collected information regarding computer science in a systematic manner.

VI. Development of Appreciation (Appreciation level)

Objectives: The learners develop appreciation of the systematic, precise and scientific dealing in the contribution of computer sciences.

Specifications: The learners

1. Realize the importance of computer science in human progress
2. Appreciate the social value of computer science as a discipline
3. Eagerly observes and approves all the desirable developments in the computer science
4. Derives pleasure in understanding the advance of computer science in all areas of human life
5. Shows respect and admiration to great scientists
6. Realize the range of magnitude from the vastness of space and time, speed and accuracy on the one hand and the minuteness space research and universalisation.

Writing Objectives in Behavioral Terms

Recently the statement of objectives in behavioural, or performance terms i.e. in terms of expected terminal behavior of the students has received renewed attention. It may be due to the major weaknesses of the taxonomies of objectives that they do not state objectives in terms of terminal behavior that is what the learner will be able to do or what will be their behavior at the end of teaching a particular topic or unit.

Instructional objectives are derived from learning outcomes. Thus instructional objectives can be stated by identifying the product of instruction in terms of observable performance. These outcomes have been referred to as behavioral objectives or terminal performances. Thus when we formulate instructional objectives for students we have to ensure that they are observable or measurable.

An instructional objective certainly tells us about the change(s) we propose to bring about in the student but it will be still clearer if we isolate the critical aspects of a particular change. Statements of objectives in terms of the change in the behavior of the students are called behavioral objectives. Instructional objectives can be transformed into behavioral objectives.

a. Concept of Entering Behavior

The starting point with respect to one's behavior in a process of instruction is called his entering behavior. It is that initial behavior which one is supposed to demonstrate before subjected to the process of tutoring, teaching or self instruction.

We have to make a search the level of potential in terms of learner's knowledge, understanding, application, interest and aptitudes covering all the domains of his behavior before his entry to the process of instruction. The evaluated outcomes in terms of entry behavior of the learner should be essentially stated in specific behavioral terms for the required clarity about the potential of the learner.

b. Concept of Terminal Behavior

It is nothing but a collection of the statements made through a number of instructional objectives set for the instruction of a particular topic or unit. It represents the final or the end behavior of a learner which is demonstrable by him after going through a particular piece of instruction.

We have to set instructional objectives, instructional process, and out teaching endeavors well within the terms of the entering behavioral input of the learners. A bright student in relation to his creditable entry behavior may be expected to show better output in terms of his terminal behavior or he will be more benefitted through a piece of instruction or attempt in teaching. How far our efforts have got success may then be ascertained through the testing measurement and evaluation of the terminal behavior of the learners.

Robert Mager's approach for writing instructional objectives:

Robert Mager is considered to be one of the first who described how to write behavioural objectives. According to Robert Mager, instructional objectives are best described in terms of the terminal behaviors expended from the learners. Mager has suggested three steps (or components) of writing performance objectives. They are:

1. Decide what the student will be able to do at the end of the learning activity.
2. Decide under what conditions the behavior will be developed i.e. indicate the condition(s) under which the behavior will be observed.
3. Decide what will be the expected level of performance i.e. indicate how will the student be expected to perform.

Mager's approach has adopted the Bloom's taxonomy of objectives as the basis for writing worthwhile objectives. He has sought the help of associated action verbs for stating different objectives. Only those verbs should be used which are direct and unambiguous. The following list of verbs will help understand and formulate acceptable behavioral objectives.

Verbs open to many interpretations (to be avoided)	Verbs open to proper interpretations (to be used)
to know	to write
to understand	to recite
to really understand	to identify
to appreciate	to differentiate
to fully appreciate	to solve
to grasp the significance of	to construct
to enjoy	to list
to believe	to compare
to have faith in	to contrast
to respect	to predict, extrapolate

Advantages of objective based instruction

1. It gives direction to the teachers and helps them to take wide decisions
2. It helps the curriculum planners to decide in advance the matter to be included in the curriculum, and the scope to be envisaged regarding its transactions.
3. Objectives aid in evaluation which in turn helps in refining objectives
4. The effort of the teacher is made more specific and concrete
5. It makes instruction output-oriented and helps to maximize the output of learning, normally development of desirable changes.

Development of Scientific attitude as an objective of teaching Computer Science

"Science is a process of human intellect. It is a way of thinking, a way of doing, a method of discovering new relationships in the physical and biological universe. It is also the product of the process".

Science as a Product

The basic components of the product of science are facts, concepts, principles, theories and laws. Whatever information we acquire through science forms the body of knowledge. Solution to every problem leads to the discovery of new problem and the cycle continues. As Science is dynamic in nature, scientific information is constantly being rearranged in the light of new knowledge. So every individual must be conscious of the ever-changing nature of science. There lies the importance of the development of the scientific attitude among students from the schools through different subjects.

Science as a Process

Observation, comparison, classification, communication, measurement, estimation and predication are the basic processes of science. The quality of knowledge acquired in science depends on the quality of process skills applied. Whatever may be the problem, the scientists adopt sharp observation and leading to sound and accurate knowledge and cautious and methodological procedure that help them to acquire valid and verifiable conclusions.

Science as both a Process and a Product

The domains of taxonomy of science are;

1. Knowing and Understanding (Concept domain)
2. Exploring and Discovering (Process domain)
3. Imagining and Creating (Creativity domain)
4. Feeling and Valuing (Attitudinal domain)
5. Using and Applying (Application and Connections domain)

Science as Method

Scientific method is one of the important contributions of science and hence the students of science should be taught and well-trained in this method, for training in this method is more important than acquisition of information. The scientific method has the following steps.

1. Sensing a problem
2. Defining a problem
3. Analyzing the problem
4. Collecting data
5. Interpreting data
6. Formulating hypothesis

7. Testing hypothesis
8. Drawing conclusions and generalizations
9. Applying generalizations to new situations

Science as Perseverance

The timescale of scientific action and discourse may go up from days, weeks and months to months, years and decades. The kind of person who can thrive in the world of modern science is likely to be characterized primarily by an almost superhuman level of the personality attribute of perseverance – the ability doggedly to continue a course of action in pursuit of a goal, over a long period and despite difficulties, setbacks and the lack of immediate rewards (and indeed the lack of any guaranteed ultimate rewards); with simultaneous, continuous productivity.

Science as an Attitude

Attitudes are dynamic results of experiences that act as directive factors when a child enters into new experiences. As a result, attitudes carry an emotional and an intellectual tone, both of which lead to making decisions and forming evaluations. These decisions and evaluations can cause a child to set priorities and hold different preferences. People with scientific attitude will the following attributes.

1. Open mindedness
2. Curiosity or inquisitiveness
3. Belief in cause and effect relationship
4. Ability to accept failure
5. Aversion to superstitions
6. Intellectual honesty
7. Objectivity and humility
8. Suspended judgment
9. Critical mindedness
10. Methodological way of solving problems

Teaching is the main part of educational process. Teaching is a set of activities which is designed and performed to achieve certain objectives in terms of changes in behaviour. It is the process of helping others to achieve knowledge, attitudes and skills. Knowledge can be used i.e. use of scientific knowledge for further constructing the knowledge. Scientific attitude as "Open-mindedness", a desire for accurate knowledge, confidence in procedures for seeking knowledge and the expectation that the solution of the problem will come through the use of verified knowledge. Involving the students in different activities and inquiries they gain facts, concepts along with attitudes. The use of knowledge assists in describing various objects, events and systems. The focus of education is to enable children to use and apply their knowledge and experiences to solve their problems on their own. Performing scientific activities, students collect new information and experiences, which result in the construction of new knowledge.

Outcome-Based Teaching and Learning in Computer Science Education

The distinction between learning outcomes and learning objectives is not universally recognized, and many instructors may find that the term 'learning outcomes' describes what they have already understood by the term 'learning objectives.' Some scholars make no distinction between the two terms; those who do usually suggest that learning outcomes are a subset or type of learning objective. Learning objectives, for example, may outline the material the instructor intends to cover or the disciplinary questions the class will address. By contrast, learning outcomes should focus on what the student should know and realistically be able to do by the end of an assignment, activity, class, or course.

The same goals addressed by learning objectives can be equally addressed by learning outcomes, but by focusing on the application and integration of the course content from the perspective of the student, learning outcomes can more explicitly and directly address expectations for student learning.

Outcomes-based education recently has become a major focus in teaching and learning enhancement for many fields of studies. Now Computer Science is recognized as a young growing field compared with many other sub-degree and even undergraduate programs. Recently, many educators in this field teaching in college as well as university have been recommended to redesign and restructure the program studies according to outcome-based teaching and learning approach. However, the issues related to how to define objectives and assess outcomes in this Outcome-Based Approach (OBA) continues to be a challenge among the computer science faculty who are not originally trained in techniques for setting up objectives and measuring outcomes.

In a traditional teaching of the computer science subject, both theoretical and practical contents are driven by the new innovative technology in industries. A course about computer programming is all about teaching students what a computer language can do and perform. It is rarely to have a tight relationship with what a student is expected to achieve at the end of the course. Unless the outcome is presented clearly and precisely to the students, the whole course can become useless and is a waste of time. Similar to other courses in other fields of studies, what is taught plays no meaning if a certain ability of students is not expected at the beginning of a course. That is the reason that the "Outcome-based approach" is brought forth and introduced to every educator, particularly in the field of computer science. Given this specific articulation path as the outcomes of the program studies, the method of teaching and learning including learning activities and assessments needs to have clear objectives both for teachers and students. In order to guarantee that students achieve certain outcomes, the curriculum design needs to be as specific as possible so that the expectation can be easily reached. The implementation and evaluation of a computer science program as sub-degree level are not widely studied. Our contribution to this outcome-based approach in teaching this area should be among the pioneers. Through the evaluation of this framework, it can motivate others to realize the usefulness and effectiveness in their curriculum design using OBA. With this approach, it could become easier to reach out to other fields and lead to a better development of interdisciplinary courses in computer science.

It has been widely promoted with evidences that OBA is indeed a promising direction in our education system such that student outcomes are to become a driving force and motivation of teaching and learning. As many places and countries are going through a new era of educational revolution, perhaps OBA framework is the antidote to bring the revolution to the highest success ever. No single pedagogy is yet perfect, but educators should continue to make effort to enhance the teaching and learning process. After we realize the goodness of OBA framework in our different programs at different levels, we believe that our students will continue to be trained and become potential future leaders in our society. In the future, we will continue to conduct both qualitative and quantitative research on outcome-based teaching and learning in computer science education at secondary level. OBA can be effective, and perhaps more effective approaches are yet to be found.

Tips to give your lesson in a great way

1. Clearly establish the learning objectives.
2. Provide an outline of lecture content.
3. Evaluate and improve your speaking skills; pay attention to the tones of your voice and your volume.
4. Trust your knowledge and preparation; convey key points enthusiastically and make eye contact with students. Avoid reading note cards, papers, or slides.
5. Move around. A moving object is more interesting than a static one.
6. Include as many visual aids as possible.
7. Open big with a provocative question, startling statement, personal anecdote, powerful quote, unusual analogy, or relevant news.
8. Plan activities that break the lecture and briefly allow students to interact and think critically.
9. Use stories from your experiences as a massage therapist to illuminate key concepts. Students love to hear about life in the real world of massage.
10. Finish forcefully by drawing conclusions and summarizing ideas. Ask students to describe what they've learned and how that knowledge will influence their practice.

In conclusion, Instructional objectives are the milestones to achieving the ultimate goal of education. In the light of the objectives, the teacher tries to modify the students' behavior with the help of tools (curriculum and other pedagogic activities) in the desired direction and ultimately the all-round development of their personality takes place. This, as we know, is the ultimate goal of education in every society. The basis for the formation of objectives is many and varied. Knowledge, individual's needs and society's priorities are the main sources for formulation of instructional objectives. It is essential to classify the objectives so that we may understand and use them properly and achieve the ultimate goal of education.

PRINCIPLES AND MAXIMS OF EFFECTIVE TEACHING

Teaching – learning process has occupied an important place in the field of Education. Teaching and learning are two fundamental aspects of educational process. Both are closely related to each other. One cannot be divorced from the other. The most important objective of teaching is to facilitate learning. Thus the concept of teaching is incomplete without learning. In traditional concept teaching is the act of imparting instructions to the learners in the class-room teaching. In traditional class-room teaching the teacher just gives information about the concept, but this traditional concept of teaching is not acceptable to the modern educators. Now teaching is not merely imparting knowledge or imparting information to the students. While imparting knowledge teacher should keep in mind the pupil as well as the orderly presentation of subject-matter.

In modern concept teaching is to make the pupil to learn and acquire the desired knowledge, skills also desirable ways of living in the society. It is a process in which the learner, teacher, curriculum and other variables are organised in a systematic and psychological way to attain some pre-determined goals.

General Principles of Successful Teaching

1. Principle of Definite Aim

Teaching should start with a definite aim. In the absence of the definite aim the teacher might go astray and at the same time his teaching might lack coherence and definiteness. The students do not gain much if the lesson is planned haphazardly and aimlessly. Without definite aim, even the best lesson would fail to achieve its objective. Definite aim is of great help to both the teacher and the taught. It makes the teaching and learning interesting, effective, precise and definite.

2. Principle of Activity

Teaching is ineffective if the students do not actively participate in the lesson. Learning becomes active and quicker if the student is made active physically as well as mentally. Teaching can be facilitated if the students actively participate in the learning process and learn while actually manipulating the things to be learnt. Student learns their best through self-activity but that activity must be psychologically sound. Learning by doing removes the dullness of the lessons and puts the children in life situations. The student engages himself fully in the activity and learns qualitatively as well as quantitatively. Only that knowledge becomes a part of the life, which he gains through self-activity. Hence teaching should be organised as to provide the maximum opportunities to the child to learn by doing.

3. Principle of Motivation

Principle of motivation is considered very important to carry out successful teaching-learning process. It is said that half the battle is won if the students are truly motivated for the lesson. Motivation is the petrol that drives the mental engine. Motivation not only promotes but also facilitates learning. It arouses the interest of child and once he is genuinely interested, he becomes attentive, and consequently learning becomes effective. Hence teacher should properly motivate the students by creating interesting learning situations.

4. Principle of Co-operation

Successful teaching is a co-operative affair between the teacher and the students. If there is no co-operation, there may not be good teaching. Hence a teacher should plan his teaching to give the pupils abundant opportunity for co-operation in organisation, management, participation in discussion, and other class-room activities.

5. Principle of Creativity and Recreation

Successful teaching is a source of happiness to the teacher and the taught as well. Work becomes its own reward for the teacher, and the students enjoy it to the maximum. Teaching is not to be continued as a routine affair. It should arouse the creativeness in the children. Successful teaching proves to be a source of creativeness and recreation. It awakens in the learners the desire to be creative and engages them in activity which is a source of pleasure to them.

6. Principle of Suggestiveness

Good teaching proceeds on the basis of suggestion rather than dictation. The military spirit is not advantageous for well conducted classroom. The teacher suggests activities, materials and modes of responses. Suggestion helps in securing co-operation of pupils. Good teachers do not give order, they give suggestions, and the students obey it. Hence in good teaching a teacher gives his suggestions to the students for doing a thing or not doing a thing.

7. Principle of Progressiveness

Teaching should be progressive. A good teacher is concerned with the progress of the children in the development of attitudes and interests, ideas and information, skills and abilities and development of habits of thoughts and action. Good teacher looks for the improvement. Progress in method and technique should find place in good teaching. Good teaching looks forward for improvement in the light of new experiments in the field of teaching. When teaching improves steadily, it is progressive.

8. Principle of Correlation

Good teaching makes the students feel everything for better life. A good teacher tries to correlate his teaching with life and one subject with various other subjects which the students are expected to study. This will make the students' whole studies interesting for them and they get the sort of feeling that the different subjects are preparing for him better life.

9. Principle of Planning

The teacher come prepared with everything planned before entering into the class. He tries to foresee the problems and thinks of their possible solutions. Thus the principle of planning helps him to perform his duty of teaching excellently. A good teacher keeps his planning flexible throughout. He may mould things here or there according to the need and requirement of the learners in different situations.

10.Principle of Individual Differences

In any group, not two individuals are exactly same. There will be always variations as far as likings and dislikes, attitudes and aptitudes are concerned. The teacher teaching the whole group by using one and same method will fail miserably. A good teacher expects the individual differences among students. He tries to satisfy one and all by using different tactics and strategies of teaching.

Maxims of Teaching

Maxims of teaching deserves more careful consideration of the teacher to enable him to make the teaching and learning go forward. Practical application of these maxims is a must for effective and efficient teaching and is indicative of teacher's ability. Utility of the maxims of teaching may be understood as follows:

1. Simple to complex

It is a well known maxim of teaching and this is the natural process of mind. It is also psychologically successful method. Classroom teaching is formal where the teacher try to teach the simple things first and the students try to learn. The teacher divides the subject matter in such a way that the simple aspects should come first there should be followed by the complex one in an order. By learning simple things, they feel encouraged and gain confidence. On that basis, they become further receptive to complex matters. If complex things are presented to the learner first, he becomes upset, bored, and finds himself in a challenging situation for which he is not yet ready being immature and ripe.

2. Known to Unknown

It is always better to proceed from known to unknown. It demands that the teacher should make efforts to establish some association with the previous knowledge of the students while imparting them any new knowledge. This maxim is based on the assumption that the student knows something. We have to increase his knowledge and widen outlook. We have to interpret all new knowledge in terms of old. Known is trustworthy and unknown cannot be trusted. Those small and simple information with which the pupils is already familiar, should be made basis for imparting unfamiliar information. The new knowledge of the unknown should be given on the basis of whatever the pupils know. So while teaching, a teacher should proceed from known and go towards unknown.

3. Concrete to Abstract

Concrete things are solid things and they can be visualized. But the abstract things are only imaginative things. So it is rather difficult to teach the children about abstract things. The students are likely to forget them soon. The mental development of the pupils begins with the concrete objects and afterwards he gains micro-words for them. Therefore, the concrete object and fact should be made known first. When knowledge about small things is to be imparted to the pupils of lower classes to provide a definite shape to their ideas, the same objects or their models, pictures, and lines should be shown.

4. Particular to General

It is always better to cite some specific example before proceeding to general principles of a phenomenon. It helps the students to follow things easily and properly. The specific example should be presented before the pupils first and then the general laws or principles should be derived from the specific examples. The teacher should present some specific examples before the pupils. Then the same example should be evaluated and after understanding the fact, pupils should be motivated to derive general principles.

5. Analysis to Synthesis

Analysis is the approach for understanding and synthesis is for fixation. By analysis, we mean breaking a problem into convenient parts while synthesis means grouping of these separated parts into one complete whole. Initially, the knowledge of pupils is vague, uncertain and unorganized. To make his knowledge clear, definite, and well-organized, we use this maxim. Analysis is dividing a problem into such living components which on assembling them may solve the problem. In analysis, the problem is separated into various elements and then these are studied. Synthesis means to understand by connecting the knowledge acquired from the analysed and living components of a problem.

6. Empirical to Rational

Empirical knowledge is based on observation and firsthand experience. It is particular, concrete and simple. We can see, feel and experience it. On the other hand, rational is based on our arguments and explanations. The stage of arguments is the last where as seeing things and feeling them is the first stage. Empirical is less general statements where as rational is more general statements. So the safe more is a teacher should proceed from empirical to rational. It is less mental maturity to more mental maturity.

7. Induction to Deduction

Induction means drawing a conclusion from a set of examples where as deduction is its opposite. Both of these approaches have their own importance. However in general, inductive approach is considered a better one.

8. Psychological to Logical

It means to follow a sequence from psychological to logical while providing knowledge to the pupils. According to psychological order, the knowledge about some object or subject should be presented according to the age of the pupils, curiosity, interests, needs and acquiring power. Contrary to this, logical order means, the present action of knowledge before pupils after dividing it logically into various units. While presenting the knowledge logically, the pupils' interest, the age and acquiring power are over-looked and only logical presentation of the subject matter is emphasized whether the pupil understand it or not. The presentation of the knowledge is psychological order or sequence is better more useful instead of teaching in a logical manner.

9. Actual to Representative

Presentation of actual things gives the children a concrete learning and thereby learners are able to retain it in their minds for quite a long. Representative things in the form of pictures, models etc. should be used for grownups who are already familiar with actual objects, where as in lower classes strictly first hand information must be given.

10. Near to a far

Every child is able to learn well in the surroundings to which he belongs. So the child would be acquainted fully with the immediate environment. Gradually he may be taught about those things which are far from his immediate environment. This type of teaching will be incremental and step by step.

11. Whole to Part

Such a method is more scientific and psychological and the knowledge acquired in this way is more stable. We gain knowledge about the 'whole' first and then about the 'parts'. It is essential to study the background and environment of the object about of which the knowledge is to be gained. Hence the teacher should present the teaching matter as a whole and in an organized way first, and then its part should be explained on the basis of this 'whole' and organized teaching-matter.

12. Definite to Indefinite

Definite things should be taught first because the learners have faith in them. Gradually he should be given the knowledge of indefinite things. Through concrete and definite examples we can have a better idea of abstract and indefinite things. It is psychological fact that the pupils' intellectual development proceeds from indefinite to definite. As the pupil grows his senses develop, through these sense organs, he goes on gaining the knowledge regarding different objects while living in the contact of his parents and other family members and surrounding social environment. On the basis of his gained knowledge, he gradually develops his personal concepts regarding objects. These concepts of ideas are vague, unclear, and uncertain. The teacher should provide certainty to the uncertain knowledge of the pupils by using concrete objects, pictures and examples.

13. Easy to Difficult

In determining what is easy and what is difficult we have to take into account the psychological make-up of the child. The interest of the child has also to be taken into account. The teacher teaches in his lesson in order of ease of understanding them. Students' capacity and standard must keep in view. This will help in sustaining the interest of the students.

14. Seen to Unseen

The pupil should be made aware of those things which are perceptual before them and then those things to the pupils ranging from 6 to 14 are at perceptual level only. Hence first of all the knowledge of present should be imparted to the pupils and the knowledge of the past and future. The teacher should use the seen or perceptual things to impart the knowledge regarding unseen or non-perceptual things. This facilitates the necessary knowledge concerning non-perceptual things.

All the above maxims helps in lesson-planning and guide the pupils keeping in mind the interests, attitudes, capacities and various levels of development of pupils. If the teachers especially student teachers want success in teaching task, knowledge of maxims is essential for them.

Principles of Computer Science Curriculum Designing

1. Focus on underlying scientific principles
2. Develop student familiarity with abstraction, complexity, modularity, reusability
3. Focus on problem solving and critical thinking
4. Help students develop a range of capabilities/skills independent of technologies
5. Give a broad overview of the field (history, computing in other disciplines)
6. Deal explicitly with design, maintenance, and analysis
7. Enable students to scaffold new ideas, concepts, and skills across a series of courses with age-appropriate outcomes
8. Use teaching strategies that make the content engaging to all students
9. Interweave conceptual and experimental issues
10. Don't confuse computer science with computer literacy.

Qualities of Exemplary Computer Science Teachers

1. **Scholarship and Professional Qualification:** A computer teacher may face with many problems, if his knowledge is not broader than the subject matter that he teaches because of the sound knowledge of the student community in the subject as well as the vast and extensive subject that he has to teach.

2. **Problem-solving Approach**: Exemplary computer science teachers use a problem solving approach that allows students to examine problems from different angles and perspectives and formulate solutions.

3. **Real World Focus and Relationship with society**: Exemplary computer science teachers motivate students by having them create real-world artefacts with an intended audience and encouraging them to understand the essential link between the problem, the user, and the solution.

4. **Explicit Emphasis on Design:** Exemplary computer science teachers explicitly teach and use the software design process, ensuring that students master the steps involved in designing, creating, testing, and debugging software.

5. **Emotional Quotient and a Welcoming Environment**: Exemplary computer science teachers make their classroom a welcoming environment for all students

(especially young women and minority students) and find creative ways to engage all students with examples and exercises that are relevant to their lives.

6. **Modelling Life-long Learning**: Exemplary computer science teachers serve as role models for their students by continuing to enhance their own teaching and technology skills and by exploring new ideas and new technologies.

Systemic Changes needed to Improve Teaching of Computer Sciences

1. **Mastery of Knowledge**: New computer science teachers should be required to have completed an undergraduate degree in computer science or a comparable degree program.

2. **Standardized Pre-service Programs**: All teacher preparation programs should be required to adhere to the National Council for Accreditation of Teacher Education (NCATE) standards for high school computer science educators.

3. **Certification standards**: State teacher certification requirements for high school computer science teachers should adhere to a consistent (and enforced) national standard that would allow for greater clarity and mobility from state to state.

4. **Professional Development**: School districts should provide regular professional development for computer science teachers to allow them to keep their knowledge and skills current.

5. **Focus on Teaching**: School districts should employ a sufficient number of technical specialists with responsibility to ensure that computer hardware, networks, and software is maintained, freeing teachers to concentrate on their teaching.

6. **Competitive Compensation:** Salaries for computer science teachers should be commensurate with those offered in industry to ensure that the best possible candidates prepare and apply for teaching positions.

7. **Professional Affiliation**: All high school computer science teachers should be members of professional associations that support their discipline-based knowledge and provide a teaching community that mentors and celebrates them.

Implementation Requirements of Computer Science Curriculum

1. **Support:** The initiative must have top-down and grassroots support and agents must be in place at all levels to ensure continued enthusiasm and support.

2. **Stakeholder buy-in**: External groups must have a role in the review process (teachers unions, professional associations, parent councils, universities/colleges and business/industry).

3. **Resources:** Schools, teachers, and students must be provided with the resources they need for successful implementation (hardware, software, textbooks, reference materials, manipulatives).

4. **Professional development:** Teachers must receive training to allow them to master the curriculum content and effective teaching strategies.

5. **Timeframe:** Every step takes time and real system change takes up to ten years. Giving less time than truly needed to accomplish any step along the implementation path from vision to reality can condemn the entire process to failure.

Creating a community of individuals and organizations working together to address issues in computer science education.

1. **Promote a Better Understanding of Computer Science**: Provide visibility, influence policy, and generate resources that illuminate computer science as an essential academic discipline.

2. **Develop Research and Resources**: Conduct original research and serve as a direct-to-practitioner channel for the dissemination of research and resources that addresses current knowledge gaps.

3. **Support National Standards**: Facilitate the implementation of national curriculum and teacher certification standards to support consistent excellence in learning and teaching.

4. **Support Teacher Excellence**: Provide multiple levels of professional development to improve teachers' technical knowledge and pedagogical skills.

5. **Opportunities**: Promote computer science as a field of study and as a career destination that provides a wealth of opportunities to students regardless of their gender, race, or socio-economic status.

As a computer teacher, our daily tasks will depend mostly on the age and ability level of our students. Younger classrooms will focus on keyboarding and understanding basic word processing and other typical office programs, as well as Internet basics. With older students, we might offer more advanced classes in software programming, hardware, web design and programming, data processing or more advanced office programs. Laboratory experiments for technology education students can be more complex and might involve one or more of these like, animation, automotive technology, computer programming, digital photography, electronics, lasers, multimedia applications, robotics etc.

Depending on the schools they teach in, technology or computer teachers might present class instruction or individualized exercises using a teacher presentation system linked to computer workstations. Computer science teacher education will emphasize math, science, communication and teaching concepts as they relate to the grade level(s) you plan to teach. Specific course work may cover the areas like, General Physics, Multimedia Design, Writing and Communication, Engineering Maths and Design, Structures and Mechanics, Manufacturing Systems, Multiculturalism, content and methods, student teaching and so on.

UNIT – IV

PLANNING AND PREPARING FOR INSTRUCTION

Effective computer science learning does not happen in isolation. Using a computer science topic as a central focus can help students see their world through the eyes of a scientist. It can provide a meaningful context in which to apply and strengthen skills already acquired and to learn new skills in different subject areas. This is a complex process involving the teacher, pupils, and a set of tasks meant for bringing about desirable behavioural changes. The success of such a venture depends on the systematic planning made by the computer science teacher.

Planning for instruction is the framework on which effective teaching is based. Careful and thoughtful planning allows instructional time to be maximized, standards to be addressed, prior knowledge to be activated, misconceptions to be confronted and the diverse characteristics and learning needs of the students to be considered. Classroom management issues are minimized and the focus can be on instruction and increasing student achievement. In addition, instruction can be scaffolded more effectively and assessments, learning goals, and content can be aligned to maximize understanding.

The Benefits of Planning

1. Creating a plan increases teacher awareness of curriculum outcomes and student needs, and enhances teaching practices.

2. Teachers are more likely to effectively meet the expectations of the curriculum, school, students, and parents.

3. Topics can be sequenced in a logical way, providing important linking for students.

4. Planning well gives teachers confidence. It enables the teacher to anticipate and be prepared for meeting individual student needs and alternative situations that arise in the classroom.

5. Planning well reduces many management problems in the classroom.

6. Advance planning helps teachers to access resources, and it reduces stress and increases effectiveness.

7. Planning well ensures a sound rationale is evident and ready for presentation to parents, students, and administrators.

8. Collaborative planning allows teachers to engage in professional dialogue about curriculum, successful practices, individual student needs, and effective use of resources.

Developing Plans

In developing plans, teachers need to effectively

1. read and understand the general and specific outcomes provided in the computer science curriculum
2. consider student needs, background knowledge, and experience
3. select the appropriate outcomes and the sequence in which they will receive focus
4. select teaching and learning activities
5. select learning resources
6. consider assessment and evaluation
7. select an approach to planning

Approaches to Planning

There are several approaches to planning for instruction. These may be categorized as thematic, integrated, content/subject based and task-based approaches. These are not mutually exclusive and often elements of each will be used by teachers to plan for instruction.

Thematic approaches focus on a specific topic or central idea which forms the basis for the unit or the lesson being planned. The theme chosen serves as the organizer for the instructional activities. Themes may be broad or may be specific in nature. School-based themes provide an opportunity for cross-subject and classroom collaboration.

Integrated approaches are closely related to thematic approaches. They focus on choosing themes that allow for connections with various subject areas or for drawing on a broad range of skills and concepts. Integrated units allow for collaboration between subject area teachers. Students may value integrated learning experiences because they are more real-life in nature and relate to other school subjects.

Task-based approaches focus on the engagement of students in very meaningful tasks rather than elements of language. Generally, in task-based approaches, learning tasks have a clear beginning and end.

Regardless of the approach or combination of approaches one may prefer, all of them may be applied to the development of yearly, unit, or lesson plans.

The Concept of Planning for Balance

Planning for a balanced Computer Science program needs to take the following into account:

1. Specific outcomes stated are end-of-year outcomes; while students may reach the level of competence described by the outcomes at any time during the year, the outcomes describe end-of-year performance. Educators must consider the series of instructional steps that will lead to accomplishment of the outcomes by the end of the year.

2. Learning is recursive and integrative. Many of the outcomes need to be addressed repeatedly in different ways throughout the school year. Students need practice in many meaningful contexts to consolidate new knowledge, skills, and strategies. As well as developing new literacy skills and strategies, students need to review, maintain, and refine those learned previously.

3. Planning is continual and informed by needs that become evident through classroom assessment.

4. A variety of instructional approaches, classroom management techniques, assessment practices, tools and strategies, and language arts learning experiences are essential.

5. Students may be taught in a variety of organizational structures, including multi-graded classrooms.

Developing a balanced, integrated Computer Science program is a creative process. Instruction is shaped by the teaching style, resources, and strengths of each teacher, by the interests, abilities, and talents that each new group of students brings to the classroom, and by the needs of the community. Planning for balance while ensuring sufficient instruction and practice in all the outcomes defined for a particular grade or course is a challenging task. Choosing particular ideas and strategies precludes using others. It is unlikely that a teacher would use all the suggestions for instruction and assessment for a specific outcome with a particular grade.

Types of Planning

Year Planning

Year planning is a long term planning of the instructional process. Year plan in a subject indicates the course purpose and objectives, course units, number of lessons, the time schedule dealing with each unit, suggested methods of teaching, details of teaching aids, their sources etc. Long-range planning is problem solving in instructional process. Long range plans are often viewed as a finished product rather than a working document and as a "means to an end." If planning is to be effective and of value to the teacher, risk taking, continual monitoring, and subsequent modifications are valued parts of the process. A real year plan will reflect changes and will be a working document, not a polished masterpiece.

Importance of Year Planning

1. A year plan is a clear indicative of the total weightage to be given for instructional objectives and content.
2. It gives the way of achieving these objectives and the methods and approaches to be adopted for each topic.
3. It gives suggestion to make teaching interesting, economic, effective and time bounded.
4. It makes evaluation easier based on the content and objectives.
5. It makes evaluation objective-based.
6. It promotes professional cooperation and mutual exchange of the ideas as all the teachers of a school plan for the year jointly.

Format of Year Plan

There are a number of formats for developing and recording an annual plan. Generally, it should be one page that clearly and concisely outlines topics and skills on a timeline.

Format 1

Date:	June	July	August	September	October	November
General Outcomes						
Specific Outcomes						
Learning Activities						
Assessment Activities						
Resources						

Format 2

No	Units	Time required in periods	Month when planned to teach	Special methods if any	Preparation and Aids necessary	Percentage of objectives to be achieved (%)						
						Knowledge	Understandin	Application	Skills	Interest	Attitude	Appreciation

Unit plan

Unit plans are more detailed outlines of the broad pieces of learning that make up a yearly plan. Teachers need to know their students, and use professional judgement and creativity to develop a unit plan that is focused, meaningful and relevant. Specify what needs to be in place for the unit to be a successful learning experience. Consider resources; allocated time; information preparation; vocabulary; instructional strategies; provisions for students with special needs; and home, school and community connections. Start with the end in mind, and build in a range of assessment activities throughout the unit. When possible, collaborate with colleagues to develop and share units. Plan ways to extend learning for students who demonstrate higher level expectations and to support those who need additional guided practice or reinforcement

Without unit plans, instructors tend to focus on class activities that may not address computer science standards. Unit planning focuses the learning on the computer science standards that are integrated thematically and practically. Lesson plans aligned with the unit are connected and spiral instruction, so that learners have multiple opportunities to develop and apply what they have learned. Without unit plans, students and instructors can become frustrated because they may see the intended progress. The objectives and outcomes in a unit plan help the instructor articulate to the students what they will know and be able to do in a specific period of time.

The following steps provide a list of considerations for unit planning:

1. Choose a theme or a topic which is of interest to the students, which offers possibilities for developing the students' computer science competence, and which allows for some general learning as well. Students can participate in this step of the planning process.

2. Decide on a unit task that is appropriate to the theme, is of interest to the students, and is within their capabilities, both from a cognitive and a practical point of view. Students can participate in this step as well. This task becomes the main element around which the unit is organized. The unit task will most often take the form of a project that can be worked on over a period of several weeks.

3. Look for resources which might be useful in preparing students to carry out the task. Resources should be attractive and rich in visual supports such as charts, pictures, diagrams, etc. Once the resources have been found, analyze them for elements that might need to be introduced, for example.

4. Analyze the task to determine what the students will need to know and to learn in order to be able to carry out the task. Think about the product the students will produce (the project or task), but also about the process they will go through in producing the product. Think about the resources we have found for the unit.

5. Outline a series of steps or mini-tasks directly related to the unit task to help the students learn and practise they will need to carry out that task. Some of these mini-tasks might focus on particular applications.

6. It is a very good idea to begin a unit with an activity that stimulates the students' interest in the topic, and helps them make connections between what they already know about the topic and what they will be learning. This introductory activity also starts to establish the linguistic base necessary for the rest of the unit, although it should not include the formal teaching of a pre-determined list of ideas.

7. It is also very helpful to end the unit with an activity that leads students to reflect on the unit. This can include discussion about what they learned, the strategies they used, and how their attitudes may have changed. It can also include planning for future units based on perceived gaps in their knowledge and skills. This step is important for developing meta-cognitive strategies and independent learning.

8. Determine the specific objectives for the unit, keeping in mind all four components (applications, computer competence, global citizenship, and strategies).

9. Think about aspects of the unit that could be adapted to accommodate the needs, interests, and aptitudes of different students. Be prepared to be as flexible as possible without compromising the objectives of the unit.

10. Plan student assessment and evaluation. Integrate assessment throughout the unit.

Unit Plan checklist

- Have you selected the outcomes you wish to focus on in this unit?
- Have you considered student needs, interests, and abilities and incorporated students' input?
- Have you considered the relevance of this unit to students' lives outside of the school context?
- Can you identify the outcomes related to language competence and applications that students will attain?
- Have you incorporated appropriate global citizenship outcomes into the unit?
- Can you identify the historical and contemporary elements of the Computer science cultures present in the content of the unit?
- Can you provide a rationale for the unit?
- Have you selected interesting, useful, and varied resources to accompany the unit?
- Have you included a variety of instructional strategies, language experiences, and activities?
- Have you provided opportunities for students to apply listening, speaking, reading, and writing skills in different contexts?
- Does the unit plan allow for flexibility and adaptation?
- Have you provided opportunities for student input and collaborative decision-making?
- Have you determined appropriate assessment and evaluation techniques?
- Have you considered possible unit extensions and applications?

Steps in Unit Planning

1. Content analysis (the what of the unit)
2. Objectives and specifications (the why of the unit)
3. Learning activities (the how of the units)
4. Testing procedures (the how far and how good of the unit)

Format of a Unit Plan

An instructional unit is essentially a complete, coherent sequence of lessons designed to cover a single topic or theme. A well-designed unit has a set of learning goals or objectives; a cohesive plan for day-by-day instruction, including some sort of introduction and conclusion for the unit as a whole; and built-in methods of assessment. The unit should incorporate a variety of learning activities, emphasize students' active participation, develop students' literacy, use appropriate materials and technology, and integrate several aspects of the content.

Subject :				Class:		
Major Unit:						
Major Objectives of the Unit:						
Sl No:	Concepts	No. Of lessons required	Learning material	Methods to be used	Aids to be used	Evaluation

Lesson Plan

Planning the instruction is much more difficult than delivering the instruction. Good lesson planning is the key to successful teaching. It is the most significant and central component of teaching task. Lesson planning is done with a view to anticipate pupil's reaction, to visualize possible learning situations, and to avoid foreseeable difficulties.

A lesson plan acts as a road map for a class session. It identifies the destination (objective of the lesson) and marks out the route (activities for each stage of the lesson). Experience will guide how detailed a lesson plan needs to be. Sharing the plan with learners keeps both the teacher and the learner focused on where they are going, how they are going to get there, and when they arrive. A lesson plan is the instructor's road map of what students need to learn and how it will be done effectively during the class time. A well-developed lesson plan reflects the interests and needs of students. It incorporates best practices for the educational field. The lesson plan correlates with the teacher's philosophy of education, which is what the teacher feels is the purpose of educating the students. It is the teacher's mental and emotional visualization of classroom activities.

According to Lester B. Stands, "lesson plan is actually a plan of action. It includes the working philosophy of the teacher, his knowledge of philosophy, his information about his understanding of his pupil, comprehension of objectives of education, his knowledge of the material to be taught and his ability to utilize effective method."

Need of Lesson Plan

1. When teachers have a readymade plan with a freedom of adaptations to accommodate all the children in the class, they are always ready.
2. One of the best ways to lower the amount of stress the teachers deal with on a daily basis is to be prepared.
3. The process of visualization will help teachers plan for and achieve a successful teaching and learning experience.
4. The teacher regularly achieves the teaching objectives and processes in a complete and perfect form.
5. It develops the possibilities of adjustment in the classroom situations.
6. It helps in planning the process of teaching on the basis of class-control, motivation and individual differences.

Aims and objectives of lesson plan

1. Specific, Measurable, Achievable, Realistic and Timely (SMART) instruction
2. Assimilation of new knowledge with already acquired knowledge
3. Giving direction to the new knowledge and subject matter
4. Realization of the general and specific objectives of the lesson
5. Analysis of the learning material, guidelines for transacting the curriculum material concerned and for evaluating the outcomes in tune with the anticipated goals.

Functions of lesson Plan

1. Provides the definite objective of each day's work.
2. Prevents the teacher from off the track.
3. As goal is fixed, teacher gets the way to achieve the goal.
4. No needless repetitions.
5. Systematic learning process in terms of pre-determined activities.
6. A sound confidence to face the class.
7. A pre-plan to make the class interesting with thought provoking questions.
8. Gives suggestion regarding learning aids.
9. Vital points are not omitted.
10. Checks unwanted experiences.

Principles of lesson plan

1. Should be a careful but flexible plan.
2. Teacher's mastery of content area.
3. Clear insight regarding methods, approaches, strategies, techniques, and models of teaching.
4. Organization of learning material based on psychological principles.
5. Active pupil participation.
6. Variety of activities to eliminate monotony.
7. Learning activities in tune with the principles of multiple intelligence.

Importance of Lesson Plan

1. If the trademark of a doctor is the stethoscope, the engineer is the calculator, the teacher cannot be able to teach without his or her lesson plan.
2. It is a one step backward two steps forward approach.
3. It gives you a bird's eye of view of things to be taught and learned everyday.
4. It provides the teacher many ways to keep the teaching process not monotonous and redundant.
5. Stick to the topic, avoid extraneous information, comments, or trivia in the lesson.
6. It can achieve definite goals and objectives
7. It prevents wastage
8. It creates confidence in the teacher
9. It creates thoroughness and effectiveness
10. It makes evaluation possible

Advantages of Lesson Planning

1. Suitable environment
2. Based on previous knowledge
3. Psychological approach in teaching
4. Limitation of subject matter
5. Determination of activities
6. Preparation of material aids
7. Means of developing teaching skills
8. Use of theoretical knowledge in teaching
9. Orderliness and development in thinking
10. Economy of energy and time
11. Flexibility and goal setting

Characteristics of a good lesson plan

A good lesson plan reflects the teacher's subject competency, knowledge of educational psychology and theories of learning, and resourcefulness in formulating learning activities. The attributes of a good lesson plan are:

1. Sound objectives, especially specific objectives
2. Thorough content analysis
3. Strong motivation strategies
4. Appropriate instructional strategies
5. Examples, comparisons related to day to day life
6. Selection of appropriate teaching aids
7. Suggested list of learning activities
8. Sufficient evaluation strategies
9. Effective black board use
10. A plan for final review
11. Prevention of indecisiveness

Essentials of writing Lesson Plan

1. Developing the Focus
2. Defining Objectives
3. Illustrating activities
4. Guided Practice
5. Getting the Feedback
6. Precise Recap
7. Individual assignments and tasks

Steps in Lesson Plan

Herbert, the first educator to apply psychology to education, and his followers emphasized five formal steps of teaching a lesson. They are;

1. **Preparation**
   In this step nothing is taught or imparted to the students. The aim of the lesson in hand automatically comes out if the teacher effectively does the preparation. A good introduction arouses the interest and stimulates the curiosity of the pupils for the new lesson. For this purpose that is to prepare the pupils to connect the knowledge to be learnt with the knowledge to be learnt with the knowledge possessed only a few questions should be asked which call for clear and concise answers.

2. **Presentation**
   In this step the teacher instead of throwing the whole knowledge to the pupils, the teacher should see that they get it steadily and assimilate it. So the subject matter should be presented in an orderly sequence after dividing it into two or more sections as the case may be. Here a lot of mental activity from the part of the students is needed. At the end of each unit, a few questions concerning that unit only should be asked to test whether knowledge has been properly assimilated and whether the pupils are now ready for the acquisition of new knowledge.

3. Assimilation

In this step, the new knowledge is to be compared, contrasted, correlated, and associated with the old knowledge. This will lead to the blending of old and new knowledge giving rise to a new and fresh truth. Here, pupils are interested when they are asked to recall what they have already learnt and associate or correlate it with the new knowledge, which is being given to them in that particular period. Through this creative process something new is made or discovered by the pupils themselves.

4. Application

It is the means of insuring knowledge and understanding. Therefore, it is essential that an immediate, simple application of the knowledge imparted should be made in the lesson itself. Here, the students are asked to write a short note or answer of certain questions concerning the lesson taught in that particular period, the students are applying the new knowledge learnt and fixed in the memory.

5. Recapitulation

It means asking the pupils to reproduce what they have learnt. It is at the end of the session, also serves the purpose of application. It looking back and surveying briefly the path that has been just covered or travelled. It connects all the essential part of the lesson in an orderly and systematic way in few minutes. It is a valuable mental exercise which makes the subject more efficient and gives increases mastery of the subject.

Lesson Plan Phases

After studying, observing, and reflecting upon lessons and lesson plans for many years, we have manipulated and adapted ideas to create a sequential design that reaches each diverse learner. Although on-the-spot modifications are almost always necessary while teaching, we use an eight-step model that engages students by building on their knowledge. The design provides many opportunities for teachers to recognize and correct students' misconceptions while extending understanding for future lessons.

Phase 1: Introduction or preparation

- Set a purpose. Describe the overarching reason for this lesson.
- Introduce the key concepts, topic, and main idea. Get students on the right track. This step may be a note on the board, a diagram, or a probing question of the day's lesson focus.
- Pull students into the excitement of learning. Seize students' attention with items like an amazing fact, a funny quirk a challenge, or other mind tickler.
- Make the learning relevant.

- Explain how this lesson extends past learning and leads to future learning—that is, the significance of the concepts, skills, and focus of the lesson.

Phase 2: Foundation

- Check on previous knowledge. Verify what students already know.
- Clarify key points. Double-check on learning from the past.
- Focus on specific standards, objectives, goals. Link the lesson to the standards, and let students know exactly what they will know and be able to do as a result of this lesson.
- Check for correctness and add to background knowledge. Add extra information for the day's learning and beyond—just enough to launch into the main lesson.
- Introduce key vocabulary. See it; say it; read it; write it.

Phase 3: Brain Activation

- Ask questions to clarify ideas and to add knowledge. Engage students in the learning and build background with probing questions.
- Brainstorm main ideas. Fill students' heads with ideas, concepts, possibilities; allow them to expand and clarify their thinking.
- Clarify and correct misconceptions. Engage students in activities that will inform you as to whether students are confused or have incorrect ideas so corrections can be made before the misconceptions become worse or detrimental to learning.

Phase 4: Body of New Information

- Provide teacher input. Lecture, add key points and new information, read the text or articles, and solve problems. Present the body of the lesson. This may be a whole-class lecture, a small-group activity with teacher supervision, or a partner activity with teacher supervision. The learning is active now.

Phase 5: Clarification

- Check for understanding with sample problems, situations, questions. Have students practice with the information just taught. Guide the learning.

Phase 6: Practice and Review

- Provide time for practice and review. Allow students time to practice under your supervision. You and the students work together.

Phase 7: Independent Practice

- Supervise students' independent practice. Select additional strategies for small groups of students who still do not understand. Other students may begin to work independently, with the final goal being that all students can work on their own. This practice prepares students for successful homework, and it prepares them for future learning.

Phase 8: Closure

- Bring the lesson to closure. Link the lesson phases and information together. Summarize the learning of the day, and discuss how it fits into the big vision for learning. Have students demonstrated what they know and can do by writing a brief note to hand in as they leave; the note may include questions, problems, or ideas on the learning. Alternatively, they may write in their journals or explain their understanding to a partner.

An Ideal Lesson Plan

Regardless of the subject we teach, making an ideal lesson plans will break the barrier. An ideal lesson plan will be;

1. Objective based
2. Appropriate material aids
3. Based on previous knowledge
4. Division of lesson plan into units
5. Simplicity of language
6. Determination of activities
7. Use of strategies, tactics, techniques, and teaching aids
8. Correlation
9. Use of illustrations
10. Individual guidance

Introspection in Lesson Plan

We cannot develop unless we are aware of who we are and what we do. Teaching practices are influenced by teachers' prior experiences and beliefs. We can take charge of our own development. Reflection is the bridge between teaching and learning. All teachers even experienced ones need lesson plans. Introspection is the best method to make lesson plan an organized one.

1. What is the nature of the lesson I am going to teach?
2. What are the objectives to be realized? Are they clear and specified?
3. Are these goals stated in terms of students' behaviour?
4. Have I analysed the curriculum material comprehensively, thoroughly and systematically?

5. Have I chosen stage appropriate, relevant and significant learning activities leading to experiences?
6. Is it possible to translate these activities into learning experiences?
7. Do I need any other input from the community resources?
8. Can I correlate this lesson to day to day life?
9. Can I approach this lesson in some other way?
10. Can I finish this lesson in time?
11. Have I considered individual differences?
12. How can I introduce the lesson?
13. How can I continuously evaluate the learners?
14. How will achieve the closure of the lesson?
15. Can this plan create motivation among the learners throughout the lesson?
16. How does this lesson fit in with the lesson already taught and likely to be taught?

Models of Lesson Plan

1. Concept Attainment Model

Concept Attainment is an indirect instructional strategy that uses a structured inquiry process. It is based on the work of Jerome Bruner. In concept attainment, students figure out the attributes of a group or category that has already been formed by the teacher. To do so, students compare and contrast examples that contain the attributes of the concept with examples that do not contain those attributes. They then separate them into two groups. Concept attainment, then, is the search for and identification of attributes that can be used to distinguish examples of a given group or category from non-examples.

Concept attainment is designed to clarify ideas and to introduce aspects of content. It engages students into formulating a concept through the use of illustrations, word cards or specimens called examples. Students who catch onto the idea before others are able to resolve the concept and then are invited to suggest their own examples, while other students are still trying to form the concept. For this reason, concept attainment is well suited to classroom use because all thinking abilities can be challenged throughout the activity. With experience, children become skilled at identifying relationships in the word cards or specimens. With carefully chosen examples, it is possible to use concept attainment to teach almost any concept in all subjects.

Name of the teacher: Standard:

Name of School: Strength:

Subject: Duration

Unit: Date:

Topic:

Curricular Objectives:

1. To identify computer as the important life and social tool.
2. To differentiate computer from all other tools.
3. To understand the parts of computer.

Process Objectives

1. Develop the concept building strategies
2. Increases logical reasoning capacities
3. Improves the analysing strategy

Definition of the Concept

Computer is an advanced electronic device that takes raw data as input from the user and processes these data under the control of set of instructions (called program) and gives the result (output) and saves output for the future use.

Attributes of the concept

Essential   : 1.

              2.

              3.

Non essential : 1.

              2.

              3.

Syntax	Teacher-pupil activity	Response
Phase I Presentation of data and identification of concept	Positive Examples Negative Examples	May be filled after the class
Phase II Testing attainment of concept	Reproduce the definition Students classify examples Teacher confirms the hypothesis Students generate examples	
Phase III Analysis of thinking strategies	Students are asked to describe the thoughts that worked in their minds while attaining the concept. They discuss the nature of hypotheses formulated, role of hypotheses and attributes.	

Social system

In the initial stages of concept attainment it is helpful if the examples are very structured. The three major functions of the teacher during concept attainment activity are to record, prompt, and present additional data. Cooperative learning procedure can also be used.

Principle of reaction

During the flow of the lesson and in later phases teacher needs to be supportive and encouraging.

Support system

Essential and non-essential attributes of examples

Varieties of labelled and unlabelled examples

Instructional effects

Students directly attain the specific concept 'computer' and improve concept building strategies.

Natural effects

Develop awareness of alternatives regarding the concepts like 'computer'. Improves sensitivity to logical reasoning in communication.

2. Advance Organizer Model

During the last twenty years this model, formulated by David Ausubel (1963), has become one of the most researched in the information-processing family. It is designed to provide students with a cognitive structure for comprehending material presented through lectures, readings, and other media. It has been employed with almost conceivable content and with students of every age. It can be easily combined with other models-for example, when presentations are mixed with inductive activity.

Teaching Manual

Name of the teacher:	Standard:
Name of School:	Strength:
Subject:	Duration
Unit:	Date:

Topic:

Curricular Objectives:

Process Objectives:

Syntax	Teacher-pupil activity	Response
Phase I Presentation of advance organizer Gives examples Provides context Prompt relevant knowledge	Teacher clarifies the aims of lesson Teacher shows the pictures Teacher prompts awareness of the students' relevant knowledge related to the content Teacher presents the material	May be filled after the class

Phase II Presentation of learning task Maintain attention Make logical order of learning material explicit	Teacher presents the material	
Phase III Strengthening cognitive organization Promotes active reception of learning	Teacher makes a conscious effort to relate the present content with the previously learnt content. Compare and contrast, analyse identical contexts, teacher clarifies doubts and queries.	

Social system

Highly structured, but requires active collaboration between teacher and learner.

Principle of reaction

Meaningfully connecting organizer and material

Support system

Presenting resources

Instructional effects

Meaningful assimilation of information and ideas

Natural effects

Develop interest in inquiry. Develop habit of precise thinking related to some specific concepts.

3. Jurisprudential Inquiry Model

It was very difficult to locate the origins of this theory. This is what we found: "Researchers Donald Oliver and James Shaver developed an approach to teaching that allows students to think systematically about contemporary issues. A replica of the judicial process, the jurisprudential inquiry approach, as it was named lets students explore controversial issues in much the same way as participants in a trial are introduced to and must evaluate or weigh evidence that is admitted. While Oliver and Shaver's teaching approach predates the performance assessment movement in American education serves today as a model for performance-based instruction with its emphasis on both process and product. In addition, many also consider the jurisprudential inquiry approach to be a model for citizenship education today". This method has been used primarily for middle school and high school social studies and science classrooms.

The six phases in this model are

1. Orientation to the case
2. Identifying issues
3. Taking positions
4. Exploring the stance
5. Refining and qualifying position
6. Testing factual assumption behind position

4. Cognitive Development Model

Cognitive development theorists generally agree that children are not passive receivers of knowledge, but instead are active meaning-makers. That is, information does not simply seep into a child's brain; children are immediately processing new ideas—putting them into categories, making connections to other pieces of information they already know, and asking questions to develop an interpretation of the world around them. This theory of "constructivism" further states that students need first-hand experience, rather than simply a teacher's explanation, to abandon preconceived notions they have. As a result, rather than always being a "sage on the stage," an effective teacher should consider when it is appropriate to be a "guide on the side," crafting activities and open ended questions that allow students to explore their world first-hand. On a cold day, younger students might believe their sweaters and hats produce heat; for some students, only through testing this notion with thermometers will the misconception be debunked. The act of watching students explore their own approaches for solving a problem—rather than simply telling them "the" way to do it, or letting them "discover" without any supervision or guidance whatsoever—gives a teacher insights into how the child thinks and how then to clarify any misunderstandings.

The phases in this model are:

1. Confrontation with stage relevant tasks
2. Inquiry
   a. Assimilation of new knowledge
3. Transfer
   a. Accommodation of new experience

70

5. Group Investigation Model

The phases in this model are

1. Encounter puzzling situation
2. Explore reactions to the situation
3. Formulate study task and organize themselves for the study
4. Independent and group study

6. Gagne's Events of Instruction

Educational psychologist, Robert Gagne, identified nine instructional events and corresponding cognitive processes that can be used to support learning. They are often used as a framework for instructional development when the acquisition of intellectual skills is the goal of instruction.

The nine events of instruction are:

- Gaining attention
- Informing learners of the objective
- Stimulating recall of prior learning
- Presenting the stimulus (content)
- Providing learning guidance (telling students the best way to learn the material you are presenting)
- Eliciting performance (opportunities to practice)
- Providing feedback (information about how to improve)
- Assessing performance (exam, tests, quizzes, papers)
- Enhancing retention and transfer (activities to help students remember and to extend the learning, transfer it to other scenarios)

7. Madeline Hunter's Seven Step Lesson Plan

These seven steps to lesson planning are often associated with the direct instruction method as well as the behaviourist school of educational practice. The seven steps fall under four categories as follows:

Getting Students Ready to Learn
1. Review
2. Anticipatory Set - focus attention, gain interest - the "hook", connect new to known
3. Stating the objective

Instruction
4. Input and modelling

Checking for Understanding
5. Check for understanding
6. Guided practice - provide feedback without grading

Independent Practice
7. Independent practice - usually for a graded assignment

8. 5 E's of Constructivism

Constructivism is a theory of learning stating that learners construct new ideas or concepts based upon their current/past knowledge. It is a very open type of planning. Faculty design instruction around a learning objective, gathers resources, and provides students with an opportunity to explore, build, and demonstrate their learning. It shifts the learning environment from one which is very instructor-cantered to one that is very learner-centred.

The 5 E's Lesson Planning Model is most often associated with constructivist learning design.

- **Engage** - students encounter the material, define their questions, lay the groundwork for their tasks, make connections from new to known, and identify relevance.

- **Explore** - students directly involved with material, inquiry drives the process, teamwork is used to share and build knowledge base.
- **Explain** - learner explains the discoveries, processes, and concepts that have been learned through written, verbal or creative projects. Instructor supplies resources, feedback, vocabulary, and clarifies misconceptions
- **Elaborate** - learners expand on their knowledge, connect it to similar concepts, apply it to other situations - can lead to new inquiry
- **Evaluate** - on-going process by both instructor and learner to check for understanding. Rubrics, checklists, teacher interviews, portfolios, problem-based learning outputs, and embedded assessments. Results are used to evaluate and modify further instructional needs.

Some Practical Considerations in Planning Lessons

A good lesson plan involves consideration of more than just what is going to be taught (the objective) and how it will be taught (materials, equipment, and activities). The following elements also need to be thought about and planned for:

1. **Sequencing**—Do the activities move logically so that learners are progressively building on what they already know? Do the activities flow well? Are transitions between activities smooth?

2. **Pacing**—Are activities in the right length and varied so that learners remain engaged and enthused?

3. **Gauging difficulty**—Do the learners have enough skill and knowledge to do the planned activities? Are the instructions clear?

4. **Accounting for individual differences**—Do the activities allow for learners of varying proficiency levels to receive extra attention they might need, whether below or above the norm? Are all students actively involved?

5. **Monitoring learner versus teacher talk**—What is the balance between learner talk and teacher talk? Does the lesson allow a time for learners to interact, producing and initiating language?

6. **Timing**—Was the amount of time allotted for each part of the lesson sufficient? If the planned lesson finishes early, is there a backup activity ready? If the lesson wasn't completed as planned, how can the next class be adjusted to finish the material?

Format of a lesson Plan

Every teacher has a unique way of completing lesson plans. Some are based on strict district guidelines, while others come out of years of experience and successful practices. There is no compulsion in the case of columns in the plan. It can be of two columns or three columns and even without column according to the convenience of the teacher. In short, importance is given not the external and physical structure or frame as done in the case of some traditional lesson plans but to the meaningfulness and effectiveness of activities.

The 4-colum lesson plan is a generally accepted lesson planning template.

Name of the teacher:	Standard:
Name of School:	Strength:
Subject:	Duration
Unit:	Date:
Topic:	

1. Concepts:

2. Specific objectives

3. Teaching aids

4. Previous knowledge

5. Introduction

6. Statement of Aim

7. Presentation

Content/ steps	Specifications	Learning experiences	Evaluation

8. Recapitulation

9. Black board summary

10. Home assignments

Example of a Computer Science Lesson Plan

Name of the teacher trainee: Unit: Date:

Name of the school: Topic:
                              Duration:

Class: Period: Strength:

Student strength:

Instructional objectives: the pupil

1. Acquire knowledge of the...........................
2. Understands the........................
3. Applies the knowledge................
4. Develops skills of........................
5. Develops interest to....................
6. Appreciates the uses.................
7. Develop attitude towards.............

Specifications: the pupil

1. Recalls the................
2. Recognizes the................
3. Classifies the...............
4. Gives reason for the..............
5. Observes the............
6. Differentiate between the...............
7. Identifies the...............
8. Locates the................

Teaching Aids: Charts, diagrams, CPU, mother board, etc.,

Specification	Content	Learning experience	Evaluation
Recalls			
Observes			
Draws			
Labels			
Locates			
Give reasons			
Identifies			
Calculates			
Classifies			
Recognizes			
Differentiates			
Showing accuracy			
Selecting accuracy			

Review
Definitions – components – characteristics – types etc.,

Assignments

1. Question 1
2. Question 2
3. Question 3

To be effective, the lesson plan does not have to be an exhaustive document that describes each and every possible classroom scenario. Nor does it have to anticipate each and every student's response or question. Instead, it should provide the teachers with a general outline of teaching goals, learning objectives, and means to accomplish them. **It is a reminder of what want to do and how want to do it.???** A productive lesson is not one in which everything goes exactly as planned, but one in which both students and instructor learn from each other.

MODEL LESSON PLAN

COMPUTER SCIENCE

Name :   Unit: Introduction to Computer   Date :

School   :

Topic: Components and Generation of Computers   Duration : 45 Minutes

Class : IX   Period: II Period   Strength :

INSTRUCTIONAL OBJECTIVES: The pupil

1. acquires knowledge of the terms – Computer, Bits, Bytes, ALU, VDU

2. understands the character of computer – parts of the computer – type of computers

3. applies the scientific knowledge to calculate the total number of bits in kilobytes

4. develops skill selecting a suitable electronic component accurately from the diagram shown.

5. develops interest to learn about different generation of computers

6. appreciates the uses of the computer in day to day life

7. develops attitude towards computer science by showing curiosity in selecting a suitable electronic component from the chart shown

SPECIFICATIONS: The pupil

1. recalls the terms – computer – Bits – Bytes – ALU – VDU – Analog and Digital Computer

2. recognizes – the components of computer – characteristics of computer – classification of computer – generation of computer

3. classifies different types of computers

4. gives reasons for input unit

5. observes the block diagram

6. draws the Block diagram

7. labels the Block diagram

8. differentiates between a) Bits and Bytes b) Analog and Digital computer

9. identifies the components of computer

10. locates the input device from the parts of computer

11. showing first generation component accurate from the diagram shown

12. selecting third generation component from the chart shown

TEACHING AIDS:
The charts showing the 1. Block diagram 2. Diagram of different electronic components used in different generation of computer, a printed integrated chip, CPU.

SPECIFICATION	CONTENT	LEARNING EXPERIENCE	EVALUATION
Recalls	Charles babbage	Who is the father of computer?	
Recognizes	Computer is an electronic machine for storing, processing and analyzing data, following a set of instruction gives to it by human.	The terms and functions of computer is learnt by the students	Define the term computer
Observes	Block Diagram	Observed the block diagram	
Draws	Block Diagram	Draws and labels the block diagram	

Labels	Diagram input unit – keyboard, mouse, scanner			Gives examples of input unit
Locates	Monitor, Printer		Locates the output device monitor, printer, floppy and CD	
Gives reasons	Gives any information to computer through the keyboard. So it is called input device		Why keyboard is called device? Given the reasons	
Identifies	Monitor, printer, floppy, keyboard		Identify a input device	
Classifies	Analog, Digital and Hybrid computer		Classifies the type of computer	
calculates	8 bits = 1 byte 1024 * 8 = 8192 bits 8192 bits = 1 kilobyte		Calculate how many bites are equal to 1 kilobyte?	
Recognizes	Analog – Greek words, it means, similarities in the form of current (or) voltage signals differential equation. Digital – operators on detached data. It process data in the digital form.		Explain Analog and Digital computer and its functions	What are the functions of Analog and Digital computer?
Differentiates	Analog	Digital	Differentiate Analog and Digital computer	What is the difference between Analog and Digital computer?
	1.requires physical analogy of Problems	Does not require physical analogy		

	2.operator by measurement of continuously varying qualities	Operator by counting		
	3. less accuracy	More accuracy		
Classifies	Generation of computer - 1st – 1946, 2nd- 1953, 3rd – 1960, 4th – 1975 5th - 1985	Classify the generation of computer	
Recognizes	1. vacuum tubes are used in 1st generation 2. transistors are used in 2nd generation 3. integrated chips are used in 3rd generation 4. speed and small in size with chip in the 4th generation of computers.	Explain different components used in generation of computer	What components used in 2nd generation?
Showing accurately	Diagram	By showing the chart, teacher asks the students to select the appropriate components of 5th generation of computer	
Selecting accuracy	Diagram	By selecting the chart student selecting curiosity of 3rd generation of computer components	

REVIEW: Computer – definitions – components of computer – characteristics of computer – classification of computers – generation of computer – types of computer

Assignment

1. Explain the generation of computer

2. What are the difference between bits and bytes?

3. Draw a block diagram, and explain the system of Digital computer.

4. Describes the components of computer.

UNIT – V

COMPUTER SOFTWARE

Computer software is a collection of computer programs and related data that provides the instructions for telling a computer what to do and how to do it. Software refers to one or more computer programs and data held in the storage of the computer for some reasons. In other words, software is a set of programs, procedures, algorithms and its documentation concerned with the operation of a data processing system.

Meaning of software

Software is a general term for the various kinds of programs used to operate computers and related devices. Software can be thought of as the variable part of a computer and hardware the invariable part. Software is the soul of the computer. Without it, the computer will never be useful and easy to use. Computer software describes different computer programs, or procedures. Software at its lowest level is called machine language, which is specific to an individual processor. Machine language is a group of binary values which basically run the computer. Software is really just an order of commands that change the hardware in a certain sequence. Normally software will be written in higher level programming languages, because it's easier for humans, unlike machine language. These higher level languages get compiled into the machine language. Or perhaps the software is written in assembly language, a representation of machine language, but by using the alphabets.

Types of Software

Software is the language of a computer. And like human language, there are many different computer languages. Essentially, computer software can be divided into four main groups depending on their use and application.

1. System software

System software performs the basic functions to start and operate the hardware components of the computer system. They instruct the computer how to operate its peripherals. In other words system software deals with running the computer system or making it work. The system software also looks after the controlling computer peripherals, coordinate the functionality of the computer peripherals, and it also manages all the computer related resources. Main functions of operating software includes (1) Management of computer's resources including optimal use of computer memory, optimize the use of central processing unit, and handle computer peripherals (2) Management of data files: loading data and program files into memory, carryout necessary tasks with computer files (3) Tasks related to management and liase with

81

user such as help user to interface with the user, select and manage input and output devices of computer, manage multitasking.

2. Programming software

It includes tools in the form of programs or applications that software developers use to create, debug, maintain, or otherwise support other programs and applications. The term usually refers to relatively simple programs such as compilers, debuggers, interpreters, linkers, and text editors, that can be combined together to accomplish a task, much as one might use multiple hand tools to fix a physical object. Programming tools are intended to assist a programmer in writing computer programs, and they may be combined in an integrated development environment to more easily manage all of these functions. Programming software usually provides tools to assist a programmer in writing computer programs and software using different programming languages in a more convenient way. The tools include text editors, compilers, interpreters, linkers, debuggers, and so on. An integrated development environment merges those tools into a software bundle, and a programmer may not need to type multiple commands for compiling, interpreter, debugging, tracing, and etc., because the integrated development environment usually has an advanced graphical user interface, or GUI.

3. Application software

Application software allows end users to accomplish one or more specific (non-computer related) tasks. Typical applications include industrial automation, business software, educational software, medical software, databases, and computer games. Businesses are probably the biggest users of application software, but almost every field of human activity now uses some form of application software. It is used to automate all sorts of functions. Computer games are the most popular forms of application software. Industrial automation, databases, business software and medical software prove to be of great help in the respective fields. Educational software is widely used in educational institutes across the globe.

4. Utility software

Utility System is system software designed to help analyze, configure, optimize or maintain a computer. A single piece of utility software is usually called a utility or tool. Utility software usually focuses on how the computer infrastructure (including the computer hardware, operating system, application software and data storage) operates. Due to this focus, utilities are often rather technical and targeted at people with an advanced level of computer knowledge - in contrast to application software, which allows users to do things like creating text documents, playing games, listening to music or viewing websites.

Functions of Computer Software

We are aware of the role of computer software in operating and managing the hardware resources of a computer. Further the application software, the prewritten set of instructions to carryout specified tasks, can perform the task as per the instructions given by the program as planned. Software can make the computer to compare data, make logical decisions, do mathematical calculations, store and retrieve data and instructions from primary or secondary memory and carryout sequence of tasks.

Computer software acts as a bridge between hardware of a computer system and the users of a computer. They enable computer user to obtain what they need from the computer. Further they make the computer to work towards giving the outputs in the manner the user wants it, such as output on a screen, makes printouts, sound, send emails or facsimiles, etc. Therefore software enables user to interact with the computer.

Much software used today are closer to English language for the comfort of the user, but the computer may not understand it since it can only understand its primary language, that is the machine language. Programmers use various secondary computer languages to develop software for different user requirements. Therefore many of the software developed by programmers need translating into the machine understandable format to execute. The translations required are carried out by another set of softwares called 'compilers' or 'interpreters'. Different programming languages need different compilers. They translate the programs written in secondary languages into machine language. Therefore the secondary languages become machine independent.

Procedure for acquiring software

1. Obtaining free software

Computer software comes in three different flavours: freeware, shareware, and commercial software and so on. Freeware is free to use and does not require any payment from the user. Shareware is also free to use, but typically limits the program's features or the amount of time the software can be used unless the user purchases the software. Free software is a software that can be used, studied, and modified without restriction, and which can be copied and redistributed in modified or unmodified form either without restriction, or with restrictions that only ensure that further recipients have the same rights under which it was obtained and that manufacturers of consumer products incorporating free software provide the software as source code. The word free in the term free software refers to freedom and is not at all related to monetary cost.

2. Shareware software

Shareware software too comes under copyright and the acquisition will only give you the license to use it, not the ownership. The conditions of license agreement vary from program to program. Shareware software licenses stipulate that, even if one archival copy of the software can be made, the backup copy cannot be used except when the original package fails or is destroyed. Modifications to the software are not allowed. Decompiling (i.e. reverse engineering) of program code is not allowed without the permission of the copyright holder. Development of new work built upon the package is not allowed without the permission of the copyright holder. Selling software, as shareware is a marketing decision and does not change legal requirements with respect to copyright, which indicates that you can make a single archival copy, for which you must pay for all the copies adopted for use.

3. Public domain

Public domain software comes into being when the original copyright holder explicitly relinquishes all rights to the software. All intellectual works are being protected as soon as they are committed to a medium. For something to be a public domain, it must be clearly marked as a public domain. The public domain software copyright rights have been relinquished. Software copies can be made for both archival and distribution purposes with no restrictions as to the distribution. Modifications are allowed. Decompiling (i.e. reverse engineering) of the program code and development of new works built upon the package (derivative works) is also allowed without conditions on the distribution and / or use of the derivative work.

4. Purchasing commercial software

Commercial software requires payment before it can be used, but includes all the program's features, with no restrictions or time limits. The people purchase them because of its advantages like a wide selection, immediate access and professional quality. Most commercial software programs ask that the user register the program so the company can keep track of its authorized users. Some commercial software programs, such as newer versions of Microsoft and Adobe programs, require the user to register the programs in order to continue using them after 30 days. While most commercial software programs are sold in the physical box, many software titles are now available as downloads. These downloads are typically made available from the company's website. The user pays for the program directly on the website and instead of receiving the software in the mail, the user downloads it to his computer. Another popular way of purchasing commercial software online is simply paying for a registration key, which unlocks the features of a shareware program. This upgrades the shareware program to the commercial version, which removes any feature limitations from the shareware version.

5. Written programs with authoring software

The Intelligent tutoring system research community uses the term authoring system to refer to a computer based system that allows a general group (including non-programmers) to create (or author) content for intelligent tutoring systems. In the development of educational software, an Authoring System is a program that allows a non-programmer to easily create software with programming features. The programming features are built in but hidden behind buttons and other tools, so the author does not need to know how to program. Generally Authoring Systems provide lots of graphics, interaction, and other tools educational software needs. An authoring system usually includes an authoring language, a programming language built (or extended) with functionality for representing the tutoring system. The functionality offered by the authoring language may be programming functionality for use by programmers or domain representation functionality for use by subject experts. There is overlap between authoring languages with domain representation functionality and domain-specific languages.

6. Own programming

Many time users who get into computers, who want to learn more about computers, or who think they have a good idea for a program may wish to create their own program can make programs of their own. For users who are interested in developing their own program, there are numerous programming languages, the program one want to develop will decide what language he should learn.

Software Ethics

Software ethics is the science of morals in computer/software usage. It is honourable to follow and live by software ethics which are a set of moral rules/principles. Unauthorized, copying of software is illegal and a violation of software ethics. The copyright law protects software authors and publishers, just as investors are protected by the patent law. Unauthorized copying of software by individuals can harm the entire academic community. If it happens in a campus, the institute may have to tackle legal liability. The institution will face grievances while negotiating dealings that would make software easily available for a cheaper price to members of the academic community. Unauthorized copying and use of software, violating software ethics deprive publishers and developers of a fair return for their work. In addition, increased prices, reduction in the level of future support and enhancements can inhibit the development of new software products.

Need for Computer Ethics

Computer ethics is a branch of practical philosophy which deals with how computing professionals should make decisions regarding professional and social conduct. With the growth of the Internet, privacy issues as well as concerns regarding computing technologies such as spyware and web browser cookies have called into question ethical behaviour in technology. We need ethics for the following:

- For the data security of the computer
- For the physical security of the computer.
- For the personal security of the user.
- For maintaining individual rights and freedoms.
- For protecting individuals from harm.
- For treating all human beings as having an inherent value and accord those beings respect.
- For upholding religious, social, cultural, and government laws and norms

Cyber/Computer Crime

When Internet was developed, the founding fathers of Internet hardly had any inclination that Internet could also be misused for criminal activities. Today, there are many disturbing things happening in cyberspace. Cyber crime refers to all the activities done with criminal intent in cyberspace. These could be either the criminal activities in the conventional sense or could be activities, newly evolved with the growth of the new medium. Because of the anonymous nature of the Internet, it is possible to engage into a variety of criminal activities with impunity and people with intelligence, have been grossly misusing this aspect of the Internet to perpetuate criminal activities in cyberspace. The field of Cyber crime is just emerging and new forms of criminal activities in cyberspace are coming to the forefront with the passing of each new day.

Let us discuss some unethical practices from hundreds.

1. Hacking and Cracking

A Cracker is a computer user who attempts to break into copyrighted software or a network computer system. Sometimes this is done with intent of releasing the software so it can be used without paying royalties. Other times, cracking is to expose a system's security flaws. For the most part, crackers do their craft with the intent to steal confidential data, acquire free software, or perform malicious destruction of files.

Hacker means someone who finds weaknesses in a computer or computer network, though the term can also refer to someone with an advanced understanding of computers and computer networks. Hackers may be motivated by a multitude of reasons, such as profit, protest, or challenge. The subculture that has evolved around hackers is often referred to as the computer underground but it is now an open community.

The standard difference is that a Hacker is attacking systems and probing security vulnerabilities for fun, exploration, fame, proving that they can, discovering weaknesses which can assist owners etc. Crackers are the profit side of the coin. Their motivation is financial gain and/or to cause damage.

2. Intellectual Property Theft

Intellectual property is any innovation, commercial or artistic; any new method or formula with economic value; or any unique name, symbol, or logo that is used commercially. Intellectual property is protected by patents on inventions; trademarks on branded devices; copyrights on music, videos, patterns, and other forms of expression; and state and federal laws.

Intellectual property theft can occur in businesses when DVDs, CDs, software or written material, such as books and journals, are illegally copied or used without the permission of the rights owner, whether through official purchase, licence, or any other form of agreement. For example putting software on to more computers than the licence allows.

Although the theft of intellectual property has always been an ethical dilemma, it is rapidly becoming a crucial problem. Intellectual property infringement has reached global proportions. Recommendations for resolution of this issue include: changing societies views, finding a legal solution to share music, and increasing the protection of intellectual property through legislation. When implemented in unison, these recommendations could be effective in reducing immoral attitude towards intellectual property theft.

3. Piracy

Software piracy refers to the unauthorized duplication and use of computer software. Software developers work hard to develop solid software programs. If those applications are pirated and stolen, the software developers will often be unable to generate the revenue required to continue supporting and expanding those applications. The effects of software piracy impact the entire global economy. The reduced revenues often divert funding from product development, and result in less research and less investment in marketing.

Software is intellectual property, and is protected by copyright laws in most countries. Most software licenses grant users the permission to use the software, but the license holder does not "own" the software - they simply own a license to "use" the software. Pirating software, circumventing the copy protection, and not properly licensing the software is illegal in most of the world. And in most countries, it is illegal to violate or circumvent software copyrights. Unfortunately, due to the global nature of the Internet, it is often difficult to enforce those copyright laws. If the pirate or offender is located in a country that does not respect copyright laws, it can be difficult to enforce penalties against software pirates.

4. E-mail Spoofing

Email spoofing is email activity in which the sender address and other parts of the email header are altered to appear as though the email originated from a different source. Email spoofing is referred to as malicious activity in which the origin details have been altered so as to make it to appear to origin from a different source. Sending fake emails is usually used to convince the receiver so that he stays unaware of the real sender. Email spoofing may be effectively used to launch phishing attacks on the receivers. The attacker may also use the attack with some amplification and in addition use mass mailer to spam mail users. Infections may be propagated by the means of spoofed emails to attack victims. There are a variety of attackers who do email spoofing. The list starts from people trying to just have fun by sending spoofed messages to users. Other serious attacks are done by wrong doers to make damages to the systems.

5. Data Diddling

Data diddling is the changing of data before or during entry into the computer system. Data diddling, sometimes called false data entry, involves modifying data before or after it is entered into the computer. Data diddling involves changing data input in a computer. In other words, information is changed from the way it should be entered by a person typing in the data. Usually, a virus that changes data or a programmer of the database or application has pre-programmed it to be changed. This is one of the simplest methods of committing a computer-related crime, because it requires almost no computer skills whatsoever. Despite the ease of committing the crime, the cost can be considerable.

6. Cyber Bullying

Cyber bullying is the use of technology to harass, threaten, embarrass, or target another person. It involves the use of information and communication technologies to support deliberate, repeated, and hostile behaviour by an individual or group that is intended to harm others. By definition, it occurs among young people. When an adult is involved, it may meet the definition of cyber-harassment or cyber-stalking, a crime that can have legal consequences and involve jail time.

7. Cyber Stalking

Cyber stalking is when a person is followed and pursued online. Their privacy is invaded, their every move watched. It is a form of harassment, and can disrupt the life of the victim and leave them feeling very afraid and threatened. Typically, the cyber stalker's victim is new on the web, and inexperienced with the rules of netiquette & internet safety. Their main targets are the mostly females, children, emotionally weak or unstable, etc.

8. Child pornography

Child pornography is defined as any visual depiction, including any photograph, film, video, picture, or computer or computer-generated image or picture, whether made or produced by electronic, mechanical, or other means, of sexually explicit conduct, where the production of the visual depiction involves the use of a minor engaging in sexually explicit conduct; or the visual depiction is a digital image, computer image, or computer-generated image that is, or is indistinguishable from, that of a minor engaging in sexually explicit conduct; or the visual depiction has been created, adapted, or modified to appear that an identifiable minor is engaging in sexually explicit conduct.

9. Masquerading

Masquerading is a sophisticated form of Cyber bullying in which an individual creates a false identity and harasses another while pretending to be someone they are not. Masquerading also includes attempts to steal log-in information, then using the information in a harassing manner such as sharing it publicly.

10.Virus

A computer virus is a computer program that can replicate itself and spread from one computer to another. The term "virus" is also commonly, but erroneously, used to refer to other types of malware, including but not limited to adware and spyware programs that do not have a reproductive ability. Malware includes computer viruses, computer worms, Trojan horses, most root kits, spyware, dishonest adware and other malicious or unwanted software, including true viruses. Viruses are sometimes confused with worms and Trojan horses, which are technically different. A worm can exploit security vulnerabilities to spread itself automatically to other computers through networks, while a Trojan horse is a program that appears harmless but hides malicious functions. Worms and Trojan horses, like viruses, may harm a computer system's data or performance. Some viruses and other malware have symptoms noticeable to the computer user, but many are surreptitious or simply do nothing to call attention to them. Some viruses do nothing beyond reproducing themselves.

Cyber laws in India

The Parliament of India has passed its first Cyber law, the Information Technology Act, 2000 which not only provides the legal infrastructure for E-commerce in India but also at the same time, gives draconian powers to the Police to enter and search, without any warrant, any public place for the purpose of nabbing cyber criminals and preventing cyber crime.

The good features of the said IT Act are that it legally recognizes email as a valid form of communication in India. Also acceptance in an electronic form of any offer, culminating into an electronic contract, has also been declared legal and enforceable. The new act has recognized digital signature for the first time in Indian law. The said new law has also granted a hierarchy of infrastructure consisting of a Controller for certifying authorities, Adjudicating Officers and Cyber Appellate Tribunal.

The most distressing part of the new IT Act 2000 is its absolute trampling of cyber liberties and freedom. A police officer of the rank a Deputy Superintendent of Police has been granted unheard of powers in Cyber law history to do almost anything for the purpose of nabbing a cyber criminal. The said unrestricted power given to police officer is in the form of an absolute discretion given to the police officer to enter and search any public place and arrest any person without warrant who is "reasonably suspected" of having committed or of committing a cyber crime or if he is about to commit a cyber crime. The discretion of the police officer further extends to defining as to who is going to be "reasonably suspected" of a cybercrime. Also, the Indian Cyber law talks of the arrest of any person who is about to commit a cybercrime. It is indeed alien to Cyber law jurisprudence as to how any police officer is going to decide as to whether a person is about to commit a cybercrime. Also, the requirements of cyberspace are very different from the actual world. Most of the times, it is difficult to decide till the last moment as to whether any cybercrime is about to be committed.

Another surprising feature of the new Indian law is that it begins by granting a legal infrastructure for e-commerce without touching anything on other important legal issues for the corporate sector like Intellectual Property Rights, Domain Names, Internet Policy, Linking or Disclaimer.

Another clause of the new law takes a contrary stand from emerging global Cyber law trends relating to liability of Internet Service Providers for third party data and information. Contrary to global trends, ISPs as a matter of principle are made liable for third party data and information made available by them through their service. However, only in two exceptional cases, the ISP is not liable if the ISP proves that he had no knowledge of the commission of any offence or contravention of the provisions of the Act or if the ISP proves that he acted with due diligence to prevent the commission of any offence or contravention of the provisions of the Act. Both the two exceptions are extremely loosely defined and the same shall become one more tool of harassment of companies in the hands of the authorities.

The biggest concern about the new Indian Cyber law relates to its implementation. The said Act does not lay down parameters for its implementation. Also when Internet penetration in India is extremely low and Government and Police Officials, in general are not at all, computer savvy, the new Indian Cyber law raises more questions than it answers them.

COMPUTER IN EDUCATION

The computer technology has a deep impact on education. Computer education forms a part of the school and college curricula, as it is important for every individual today, to have the basic knowledge of computers. Computers have brought about a revolution across all industries. They have changed the face of society. They are no longer specialized tools to be used by specially trained people. They are ubiquitous and used in almost every sphere of life. Computers are the best means for storage and management of data they can serve as huge knowledge bases and can be harnessed for all sorts of financial transactions owing to their processing power and storage capacities. As computers are a daily utility, they have gained immense importance in day-to-day life. Their increasing utility has made computer education the need of the day and the teachers of the computer science as well.

Roots and Rudiments of Educational Computing

Educational computing is a diverse area of study which is concerned with the design, implementation and assessment of computer-based technologies to enhance education and training.

The huge effect of computer technologies can be seen in almost every area of our lives. Computers have increasingly been affecting education, and it seems that they will likely shape the future of education. There are many dimensions on which technology use in education has changed. Computer's use in education started as a tutor, then as a tool and now a tutee. Before reaching the current state of computer technology in education, there were some evolutionary steps. We can group the stages and ages into three major periods based on the primary technology that lead each period. These periods are: 1) Mainframe Period, 2) Microcomputer Period, and 3) Internet Period. Understanding these three periods sheds light on understanding the uses of computers in education and for predicting possible future trends in computer use in education as well.

1. Mainframe Period (Late 1950s to Late 1970s)

In the 1920s, use of instructional radio laid the foundations of machine-use in educational settings. With the introduction of instructional television in the 1950s, educational technology started to be considered as a promising field to make classrooms engrossing and generative places for learning. The impact of television on education and its role in communicating messages worldwide using images and sound were tremendous. At the beginning, there were too many expectations for radio and television. After a while, these were found to be not responding well to the actual needs and goals of education. Researcher found some missing sensory components, such as smell, taste, and touch and some researches revealed that there was not much difference between conventional classes and classes with instructional television and radio. These results were not surprising, since an important method for learning was missing in these two educational technologies. That method was interaction, which is considered a powerful tool for learning. At this juncture computers met the need for a technology that could provide an interactive environment in the classroom. They opened a new age in the history of education and affected the way students learn and these small machines made much more important impacts on education than any other machine in that time.

Beginning about 1958, the earliest applications of computers emerged as programs for teaching certain subjects. IBM's Teaching Machines Project is considered to be the pioneer implementation of this application. Initially, the IBM 650 computer was used for simulating a teaching machine, based on Skinner's (1954) programmed instruction, for teaching basics of binary arithmetic. We can rightly call this function of computer as tutor since computers were in the role of teaching a certain subject.

In 1959, an individualized instruction system called PLATO was developed by a number of scientists in the University of Illinois. PLATO was a computer-assisted instruction tool in mainframe computers. There was a single central computer and independent computer terminals for the students. Each of these terminals could interact with the central computer using a touch-sensitive screen and a keyboard. This system supported graphics, which were ideal for simulations. It also supported drill and practice, tutorials, and problem solving. The logic behind this system was simultaneous individualized delivery of computer-managed instruction.

In 1967, Seymour Papert and his colleagues developed the first version of LOGO, an important pioneer of programming tools in education, in the MIT Artificial Intelligence Laboratory. LOGO was a simplified programming language that enabled children to use various commands to 'teach' a turtle to draw objects on the screen that could be printed to a piece of paper. Throughout the 1970s, research was conducted to evaluate the effectiveness of LOGO for teaching programming skills in schools. Yet computer programming was not a predominant application of computers in education at that time on the reason that, to learn programming, even a simple language such as LOGO, takes a lot of time, and the learning gains from programming may not justify the amount of time spent learning that language.

The popularity of computer-assisted instruction continued with the development of TICCIT (Time-shared, Interactive, Computer-Controlled Information Television) around 1975. TICCIT was developed as a mini-computer system, combining computer and colour television technology. One of the most important differences was its ability to support learner control. Also, authors were responsible for providing the content to be taught, but the instructional strategy was built into the system in the form of standard strategy components. The students could choose the strategy components, which contributed to the learner control function. However, TICCIT was on a level of sophistication well beyond just drill and practice.

Around 1982, technology had started to assume an important promising role in education. Students spent only about an hour a week using computers in the schools. More importantly, the purpose of use varied significantly.

2. Microcomputer Period (Late 1970s – End of 1990s)

With the introduction of cheap desktop computers, these machines were placed at the top of the list of educational fads. After this introduction, workshops were offered to teachers to learn how to program computers and to use these machines in classrooms. Parents raised money to buy computers for their children's schools, which shows the perception and attitude of parents toward these innovations at that time.

The 1980s were a period of rapid growth of computer-based education because of the availability of more powerful microcomputers at lower cost. In 1981, when the IBM Personal Computer was released, there was an increase in demand for microcomputers in business and industry. However, having an early lead, reasonable cost, courseware availability, better graphics capability, and some other advantages, Apple II dominated educational settings. In contrast, the IBM PC started to be widely used in higher education and corporate settings.

In 1983, Apple introduced the "School bus Network" to the market, which enabled teachers to communicate with their students via a computer network. A teacher's station and students' computers were connected to each other so that the teacher could view students' work, exchange messages, and give feedback. This network application was revolutionary because it altered the traditional ways of instruction and classroom management.

In 1984, Apple's Macintosh computer was released, which changed the field of micro-computing a lot because of its unique feature of mouse input and better graphical and text support. This computer came with a free HyperCard program allowing teachers to make their own software applications and tutorials for students. However, the Macintosh's higher cost and poor availability of courseware prevented it from penetrating the educational setting much. In the Microcomputer period, computer literacy became less of an obstacle, since the availability and use of computers had increased. Strikingly, students became much more knowledgeable than their parents and even in some cases than their teachers in this period of use.

In the early1990s, many other applications of computers in education appeared. Word processing applications were a predominant form of computer use among students in this period because students could finish their work more easily than using pen and paper, and they could change the text easily. Another application was the electronic spreadsheet. Educators recognized the value of spreadsheets as being strong instructional tools beyond their number-crunching value. Therefore, students started to manipulate and analyze data in spreadsheets. Teachers were using database applications for lesson objectives focused on critical thinking skills. With the help of database management systems, students could store, organize and manipulate data for their classes.

3. Internet Period (Early 2000s - Today)

Although the origins of the Internet date back to the early 1960s, it took a while to mature and penetrate into educational settings. There was extensive availability of Internet connections in schools in 2006. Teachers used web sites during their instruction as secondary resources, while textbooks were used as primary resources. However, there was a change in focus from using computers mainly for teaching and learning to using them more for assessment, driven by the No Child Left Behind (NCLB) initiative. There was an explosion of access to content on the Internet. Teachers and textbooks no longer had a monopoly on content, and this allowed a change in the teacher's role.

With the advent of wireless technology, schools found it easier and less expensive to adopt this emerging technology. Laptops with wireless technology demonstrated a remarkable growth during 2005. Later the importance of social networks is emphasized and a significant improvement in educational outcomes resulting from academic and emotional support given by network members happened. As a form of social network, weblogs have become one of the more common ways of using technology in education in this Internet period. Blogs provided a web-based communication environment in which a group of people shares their interest about a specific that blogs became important tools to support self-expression and creativity since they look like a personal diary.

Another emerging technology in this period is "personal broadcasting". This technology is used for distributing sound or video files to users. One of the most famous applications of personal broadcasting is podcasting. With podcasts, students can share their media and have access to media created by other students. Podcasting has been growing at a rapid pace since it was introduced in late 2004. Its increasing popularity among teachers and students seems likely to continue into the future.

Data Management Systems and Course Management Systems (CMS) are other up-coming technologies in this period of use. Because of the trend to use technology for collecting and managing student assessment data, in this period Data Management Systems have received great consideration and application in educational settings. They have gained great popularity in higher education, and their use is spreading throughout.

Future of Educational Computing

To conclude, although it is difficult to predict the future of educational computing, we can foresee some of the developments that are likely to characterize the next period of educational computing, and these developments should help us in our attempts to evolve toward an ideal use of technology to support education. Current trends indicate that we should start by changing the perception about computers in education. Instead of using them as a way to enhance teacher-cantered instruction, we should make use of computers as the major tool for teaching and learning in a learner-centred environment. Moreover, changes in the needs and nature of information-age students create different needs and expectations for educational technology. Looking at society's trends today will shed light on features of an information-age educational system. We see a great need for Personalized Integrated Educational System (PIES) since it supports personalized computing for an information-age educational system.

Computer in Teaching

Technology ushers in fundamental structural changes that can be integral to achieving significant improvements in productivity. Used to support both teaching and learning, technology infuses classrooms with digital learning tools, such as computers and hand held devices; expands course offerings, experiences, and learning materials; supports learning 24 hours a day, 7 days a week; builds 21st century skills; increases student engagement and motivation; and accelerates learning. Technology also has the power to transform teaching by ushering in a new model of connected teaching.

1. Preparation for Instruction

Teaching at School as well as Higher Education, mostly, concentrates on giving information which is not the sole objective of Teaching. Along with giving information, the other objectives are: (1) developing understanding and application of the concepts (2) developing expression power (3) developing reasoning and thinking power (4) development of judgment and decision making ability (5) improving comprehension, speed and vocabulary (6) developing self-concept and value clarification (7) developing proper study habits (7) developing tolerance and ambiguity, risk taking capacity, scientific temper, etc.

With the present infrastructure, class size, availability of teachers, quality of teachers, training of teachers, etc., it is difficult to achieve all the objectives. Lecture Method which does not have potentiality of achieving majority of above mentioned objectives. The objectives are multi-dimensional in nature, so for their achievement multiple methods should be used in an integrated fashion. It is a well known fact that not a single teacher is capable of giving up to date and complete information in his own subject. The computer technology can fill this gap because it can provide access to different sources of information. It will provide correct information as comprehensive as possible in different formats with different examples. ICT provides online interaction facility. Students and teachers can exchange their ideas and views, and get clarification on any topic from different experts, practitioners, etc. It helps learners to broaden the information base. Computer Technology provides variety in the presentation of content which helps learners in concentration, better understanding, and long retention of information which is not possible otherwise. The learners can get opportunity to work on any live project with learners and experts from other countries. Flexibility is a must for mastery of quality teaching.

2. Development of Instructional Material

At present there is a shortage of qualified and competent teachers in all most all subjects at all levels. Book reading is not very enjoyable and does not help students in understanding the concepts and retaining the information. There are many teachers who are well known for the specific subject. Their lectures should be digitalized and made available to all the users. It will enhance the quality of instruction in the classrooms. The teacher can use them in the classrooms and can organize discussion after it wherein the new points can be added both by the teacher as well as students. It will make the teaching effective, participatory and enjoyable.

3. Development of Virtual Laboratory for each subject

The students understand better, if they do some practical related to the concept. It makes learning easy and interesting. Laboratory helps in developing scientific temper. But the fact is that practical are not done by each student in each school. There are many schools which do not have laboratory. Sometime if laboratory is available, the instrument is not available. The students are not given freedom to do experiments on their own. In short, there are many restrictions under which the students have to work in the laboratory. Now it is possible to have Virtual laboratory. Once the Virtual Laboratory is developed, it can provide lot of freedom to students. The students can manipulate any attribute or variable related to the experiment and can see how it affects the outcome. Suppose a student wants to study the factors that can affect the focal length of a mirror. At present in the real laboratory, the student cannot manipulate many variables that he thinks might be related. But Virtual laboratory can provide lots of freedom to the student. That is, student can take different types and shapes of objects, change the distance between mirror and object to any extent, change the thickness of the mirror, etc. and can see how such attributes affect the focal length of the mirror. The Virtual Laboratory can be developed using Computer Technology. It may be made available at the door step of each and every student by uploading it on the Website.

4. Development of Diagnostic Testing

The common observation is that the quality of teaching in the classroom is on the decline. More and more students are depending on the private tutorial classes. The private tuition also has become a business. This phenomenon is observed not only in India but in other countries too. There are students who fail to understand certain concepts or retain certain information. This can be assessed by introducing the diagnosis in the process of teaching – learning. Today, this is not being done. The reasons might be large class size, non-availability of diagnostic tests in different subjects, lack of training, money and desire on the part of teacher, etc. This is the age of technology. These difficulties can be easily over come with the help of ICT.

5. Development of Psychological Testing

There are individual differences. Through research some correlates of academic achievement have been studied. Rarely this information is used by school or college teachers. Many of them even do not know about such researches. Even if they know, they do not make use of it at the time of forming the groups for different academic activities. One of the major reasons is that the school does not have a trained psychologist who can assess the students on some of the correlates of academic achievement. Further, the psychological testing is laborious and involves money and time. Even the appropriate psychological tests are not available. This is the age of digital technology. It can be used to digitalize all the psychological tests including the scoring and evaluation. The same may be available on the website and students and teachers can use them whenever required. Even student can use it individually and can share the result with the teacher who can help the student to improve his academic performance. The digitalized psychological tests will be easy to use and economical also. Thus ICT can be used in psychological testing also.

6. Computers in Remedial Teaching

Once the Computer Technology is used for diagnosis purpose, the next step is to organize Remedial Teaching Programme. The Remedial Teaching can be done by the teacher if some common mistakes are identified. It may not be feasible to organize Remedial programme for individual students. At this point, the ICT can be used for giving individual Remedial Programme. It may be online or off line. The instructional material if designed specifically for meeting the individual needs of students and uploaded on the School website and then the ICT can be used for providing Remedial Teaching Programme.

Computer in Learning

Through the use of advanced computing and telecommunications technology, learning can also be qualitatively different. The process of learning in the classroom can become significantly richer as students have access to new and different types of information, can manipulate it on the computer through graphic displays or controlled experiments in ways never before possible, and can communicate their results and conclusions in a variety of media to their teacher, students in the next classroom, or students around the world.

1. Autonomy of Learning

It is a capacity for detachment, critical reflection, decision-making, and independent action. It presupposes, but also entails, that the learner will develop a particular kind of psychological relation to the process and content of his learning. The capacity for autonomy will be displayed both in the way the learner learns and in the way he or she transfers what has been learned to wider contexts. Computers as tutors have a role in promoting learner autonomy if the programs are well designed and have been chosen by students. Teachers can encourage learners to think about the choices they are making and reflect on how the program is beneficial. Computers as tools potentially facilitate learner autonomy more efficiently as students make more of the decisions about how to use the tool. Students still need to be helped to understand how a tool might benefit their overall learning.

2. Mastery of Self-regulation Skill

It is proved that what difficulties still remain in supporting learners' mastering of SR skill, a computer-based learning support environment to help a learner to master SR skill. This environment provides opportunities for learners to collaboratively master their SR skills gradually based on Vygotsky's socio-cultural theory: first, they learn the skill by observational learning, and then, they learn the skill by using it as a cognitive skill. Finally, they try to use the skill as a met cognitive skill with a computer system's support.

3. Computers as Mindtools

Computers can most effectively support meaningful learning and knowledge construction in higher education as cognitive amplification tools for reflecting on what students have learned and what they know. Rather than using the power of computer technologies to disseminate information, they should be used in all subject domains as tools for engaging learners in reflective, critical thinking about the ideas they are studying. Using computers as Mindtools by employing software applications as knowledge representation formalisms will facilitate meaning making more readily and more completely than the computer-based instruction now available. There are several classes of Mindtools, including semantic organization tools, dynamic modelling tools, information interpretation tools, knowledge construction tools, and conversation and collaboration tools.

4. Computers catering different Learning Styles

Although the use of computers in the classroom has been heralded as a major breakthrough in education, many educators have yet to use computers to their fullest advantage. This is perhaps due to the traditional assumption that students differed only in their speed of learning. However, new research indicates that students differ in their style of learning as well; some preferring visual information; others, auditory or tactile. A new generation of computer software that can be tailored to a student's preferences has been developed, and its use in the classroom has yielded dramatic results. For instance, Thinking Networks has developed a program designed to help improve writing skills--skills that are notoriously poor among many students. By presenting nonverbal graphic images that symbolize semantic relationships; this program is immediately accessible to many visually-oriented students. The program also develops basic thinking operations, such as sequencing, organizing, comparing, and contrasting, and can be tailored to students' preferences in a number of other ways as well. Through the thoughtful use of computers and Computer Managed Instruction, technology can serve the needs of education in a way no other tool can.

5. Enhancement of Multiple Intelligence

According to constructivist approach to learning, integrating multimedia and multiple intelligences can improve the active participation of the learner and improve the quality of learning. Humans process and gather information differently. Dr. Howard Gardner identified different styles of learning as eight distinct intelligences: logical/mathematical, interpersonal, intrapersonal, musical, kinaesthetic, naturalist, linguistic, and visual/spatial.

One challenge educators face is how to deliver materials and subject matter to learners whose acquisition of knowledge depends on their mode of learning (intelligence). Gardner argues that students would be better served if disciplines could be presented in number of ways. Simply stated, we can promote students' learning via their intelligence. Multimedia offers a medium that addresses these intelligences. Multimedia programs that incorporate sound files (MP3, MPEG, and MIDI) can improve learning for musically strong students. Logical/mathematical intelligences can be maximized using online calculators, multimedia authoring programs, or problem-solving software.

Computer in Assessment

Testing, Measurement, and Evaluation are the indicators of a quality education system. Continuous tests and evaluations are essential for the improvement in the whole teaching learning process. They are used for Motivation, Achievement, Improvement, Diagnosis, Prescription, Grading, Classification and Prediction.

Administrative concerns of Assessment are Relevance, Education value, Economic value, Time, Norms, Bias and Safety. Moreover, increased numbers of students in Higher Education and the corresponding increase in time spent by staff on assessment has encouraged interest into how technology can assist in this area. Ensuring that the assessment methods adopted reflect both the aims and objectives of the course and any technical developments which have taken place is becoming increasingly important, especially as quality assurance procedures require departments to justify the assessment procedures adopted.

Assessment consists of taking samples of behaviour at a given point in time and estimating the worth of those behaviours. Thus the underlying assumption of assessment is that it provides a representative sample of behaviour of the person being assessed. On the basis of the kind of sample taken inferences are made about a person's achievements, potential, aptitudes, intelligence, attitudes and motivations. All forms of assessment provide estimates of the person's current status. Here lies the potentiality of computer based assessments.

1. Electronic Test

Electronic assessment tools are unlikely to reduce significantly the burden of assessment, but they can be used to promote deeper and more effective learning, by testing a range of skills, knowledge and understanding. Using computers in assessment does not have to mean more multiple choices testing to the exclusion of other assessment techniques. A wide range of innovative assessment methods lend themselves to computer based implementation.

A. Electronic delivery of tests

There is growing interest and increasing practical experience in the use of computers to deliver objective tests. Objective testing is often taken to imply the use of multiple choice questions (MCQs). However, objective tests can incorporate a wide range of question styles in addition to standard multiple choice questions; for example multiple response, word entry, number entry, gap-fill and free-format where student entry is compared to a correct solution using a keyword search. Objective tests and MCQs in particular, are generally considered to be an efficient method of testing factual knowledge, enabling a wide syllabus to be examined in a relatively short time. It is, however, important for academic staff to be aware of the limitations of objective tests (especially MCQs), particularly in their inability to indicate higher level and process skills. Objective tests can be used for both formative and summative assessments, and a variety of scoring systems can be applied, tailored to the importance of discouraging students from guessing answers.

Several packages are available which are designed for the electronic delivery of objective tests (e.g. Question Mark, Examine, EQL Assessor), all of which support the delivery of a variety of question types. Entering questions is generally straightforward, requiring minimal experience with the package. Although the design of questions for computer based delivery is no more difficult than for paper based objective tests, this remains non-trivial and the most time consuming part of the whole objective testing process. Difficulties can sometimes arise where subjects require the use of specialized notation (such as for mathematics, chemistry or linguistics) but these can almost always be overcome by the use of appropriate specialized fonts, or the inclusion of small graphic objects. When the test has been completed the students' responses are marked automatically, quickly and consistently.

B.   Electronic recording and analysis of results

Perhaps the most immediately obvious and most easily accessible use of technology to assist the assessment process is in the recording, analysis, general storage and management of results. A wide range of spreadsheets, statistical packages and database packages are available (e.g. Excel, Lotus 1-2-3, Database, SPSS, Minitab, Access), into which it is easy to enter data manually if results are not already in electronic form, though enormous care must be taken to avoid transcription errors when generating the data files. Most of these packages readily accept the transfer of electronically stored data from other applications, aiding data acquisition and increasing the potential data analysis that can be carried out.

Results from several assessments, courses or modules can be collated quickly, easily and accurately for discussion at examination boards, and the volume of paper required for long term storage can be dramatically reduced. Further, any trends within the data can be fully explored, which in turn provides valuable feedback for the academic team.

C.   Electronic Scoring tools

The use of electronic methods to store and manipulate data becomes pointless if the integrity of the data cannot be guaranteed. The manual entry of marks is particularly susceptible to error, time consuming and costly to check thoroughly. The use of data capture devices, such as an Optical Mark Reader (OMR) connected to a computer, can vastly reduce input errors, particularly the problem of number transposition on data entry, e.g. typing 45 instead of 54.

Standard pre-printed OMR forms can be a cost-effective way of collecting student responses to questions. A pencil or pen mark is made on the form by the student to indicate each selected response, i.e. their answer to a particular question. No special training is required for this just some simple instructions are entering responses clearly in the designated check areas. The completed forms can then be scanned by an OMR to detect the presence of a mark usually by measuring reflected light levels. The pattern of marks and spaces is interpreted by the reader, following instructions provided by the operator, and is stored in a data record and sent to computer file for storage. Thus large quantities of information can be entered onto computer without the need to use a keyboard. Hence increasing accuracy and saving time.

2.   Computers in Measurement

Measuring student learning outcomes or SLOs is the most important measurement of educational process. It means determining if intended learning has actually occurred. Student learning includes the full breadth of education: acquisition of skills, mastery of concepts, and growth in life perspective. Learning outcomes are direct measures of learning, distinct from indirect measures such as graduation rates, course completion rates or even course grades.

When we grade a student assignment, we look for particular elements that the student has demonstrated and evaluate the extent to which the student has presented that element. The element of the answer may be present or absent and, if present, may be excellent, good, satisfactory, or unsatisfactory. Based on this analysis, we award points or grades or in some other way identify how this particular assignment contributes to the overall course grade.

To measure student learning for a comprehensive program, departments can identify a set of expected outcomes which, taken as a whole, reflect what core concepts, abilities, and values students should have upon completion of the program. Each of these outcomes should have associated measurable criteria and one or more assessment tools to gather the data. The results of these assessments should be collected and analyzed regularly. This information should be used to continuously improve student learning. In all these case the role of computer is irrefutable.

3.   Computers in Evaluation

At present the paper pencil tests are conducted for evaluating the academic performance of students. These tests are conducted in the group setting. The content coverage is poor and students cannot use them at their own. These tests are evaluated by the teachers and they may not give feedback immediately to each and every student. It may be due to this that students are unable to know their weakness and do not make any attempt to improve upon them. The ICT can be made use in the evaluation. Computer based test can be used by individual student to evaluate his learning. The student can instantaneously get the feedback about the status of his understanding. If the answer is wrong, he even can get the correct answer. It goes a long way in improving the learning and teacher has no role to play in it. It is left up to students to use it. Such tests can be uploaded on the website for wider use. The students from other institutes can also make use of it. Not only the students even the teachers can also use it to assess their own understanding of the subject. If used by teachers before teaching the topic, they can prepare the topic properly. Such software can be used for internal assessment. Thus, ICT can be used to improve the quality of pre as well as in-service teacher's training.

Computer in Guidance and Counselling

The availability of computer applications in counselling and guidance has increased in recent years. It is true that there may be counsellors at all levels of education, there seems to be little evidence of widespread adoption computer technology at any level. But, counsellors can utilize technology to make their jobs easier. Some of the benefits of counsellor utilization of technology include greater efficiency in record keeping and the automation of tasks. The benefits are not limited to the counsellor. Counselees also benefit from counsellors using technology. One such benefit is that students are usually motivated by technology use. Although the advantages of using technology are numerous, counsellors are at various levels in their adoption rates of technology in their counselling environments. There are much guidance and counselling softwares are available in the market.

Computer can be used in the following areas of Guidance and Counselling.

1. Scheduling
2. Student-record systems
3. Research
4. Records retrieval
5. Simulation
6. Follow-ups
7. Referrals

Computer in Teaching Different Subjects

Computer-assisted instruction is used through the entire range of education from preschool to professional school. It has been offered in a wide variety of fields, including all the main school subjects taught in elementary and secondary schools and it is the tool of all subject teachers.

The most interesting research on the ways technology can improve what children learn, however, focuses on applications that can help students understand core concepts in subjects like science, maths and literacy by representing subject matter in less complicated ways. The research in this area has demonstrated that technology can lead to profound changes in what children learn. By utilizing the computers' capacity for simulation, dynamically linked notations, and interactivity, ordinary students can achieve extraordinary command of sophisticated concepts. Computer-based applications that have had significant impacts on what children learn in the areas of science, mathematics, and the humanities are discussed below.

1.   Teaching of Science: Visualization, Modelling, and Simulation

Over the past two decades, researchers have begun to carefully examine what students actually learn in science courses. To their surprise, even high scoring students at prestigious universities show little ability to provide scientific explanations for simple phenomena, such as tossing a ball in the air. This widely replicated research shows that while students may be able to calculate correctly using scientific formulas, they often do not understand the concepts behind the formulas.

Computer-based applications using visualization, modelling, and simulation have been proven to be very powerful tools for teaching various scientific concepts. Involving students in making sense of computer simulations that model physical phenomena, but defy intuitive explanations, has also been shown to be a useful technique. Software applications have been proven successful in helping students' master advanced concepts underlying a variety of phenomena. Research has shown that students using the curricula demonstrate increases in both their comprehension of meteorology and their skill in scientific inquiry.

2. Teaching of Mathematics: Dynamic, Linked Notations

The central challenge of mathematics education is teaching sophisticated concepts to a much broader population than has traditionally been taught such material. This challenge is not unique to India, but almost every nation is disappointed with the mathematical capabilities of their students. Not so long ago, simple merchant mathematics (addition, subtraction, multiplication, and division) sufficed for almost everyone, but in today's society, individuals are increasingly called upon to use mathematical skills to reason about uncertainty, change, trends in data, and spatial relations.

While seeking techniques for increasing how much mathematics students can learn, researchers have found that the move from traditional paper-based mathematical notations (such as algebraic symbols) to on-screen notations (including algebraic symbols, but also graphs, tables, and geometric figures) can have a dramatic effect. In comparison to the use of paper and pencil which supports only static, isolated notations, use of computers allows for "dynamic, linked notations" with several helpful advantages, as described below:

- Students can rapidly explore changes in the notation by dragging with a mouse, as opposed to slowly and painstakingly rewriting the changes.
- Students can see the effects of changing one notation upon another, such as modifying the value of a parameter of an equation and seeing how the resulting graph changes its shape.
- Students can easily relate mathematical symbols either to data from the real world or to simulations of familiar phenomena, giving the mathematics a greater sense of meaning.
- Students can receive feedback when they create a notation that is incorrect.

3. Teaching of Social studies and Arts

Unlike science and maths, breakthrough uses of technology in other subject areas have yet to crystallize into easily identified types of applications. Nonetheless, innovators have shown that similar learning breakthroughs in these areas are possible. For example, the commercially successful SimCity game (which is more an interactive simulation than a traditional video game) has been used to teach students about urban planning. Computer-based tools have been designed to allow students to choreograph a scene in a Shakespeare play, or to explore classic movies, such as *Citizen Kane,* from multiple points of view to increase their ability to consider alternative literary interpretations. Through the computer projects students are provided access to a pioneering multimedia learning environment for exploring hyperlinked documents and cultural artefacts from ancient civilization. Similar software can provide interactive media environments for classes in the arts. An emergent theme in many computer-based applications in the humanities is the use of technology to allow students to engage in an element of design, complementing and enhancing the traditional emphasis on appreciation.

4. Teaching of Languages

It is helpful to think of the computer as having the following main roles in the language classroom:

A. Computer as a Language Teacher

In the early days of computers and programmed learning, some students sat at a terminal for extended periods following an individualized learning program. But now computer could eventually come to replace the teacher, there has been a return to a much more sophisticated kind of computerized teaching using multimedia CD ROMS. In such programs, students can listen to dialogues or watch video clips. They can click on pictures to call up the names of the objects they see. They can speak into the microphone and immediately hear a recording of what they have said. The program can keep a record of their progress, e.g. the vocabulary learned, and offer remedial help if necessary. Many of these CD ROM programs are offered as complete language courses.

B. Computer as a Tester

The computer is very good at what is known as *drill and practice*; it will tirelessly present the learner with questions and announce if the answer is right or wrong. In its primitive manifestations in this particular role in language teaching, it has been rightly criticised. The main reason for the criticism is simple: many early drill and practice programs were much unsophisticated; either multiple-choice or demanding a single word answers. They were not programmed to accept varying input and the only feedback they gave was *Right* or *Wrong*. In computerized language learning, the student is in full control, the computer is extremely patient and gives private, unthreatening feedback. Most programs also keep the score and have cute animations and sounds, which many students like. There are some programs which do offer more useful feedback than right or wrong, or that can accept varying input. Such programs blur the role of the computer as teacher or tester and can be recommended to students who enjoy learning grammar or vocabulary in this way. If two or more students sit at the same computer, then they can generate a fair amount of authentic communication while discussing the answers together.

C.   Computer as a Tool

Spreadsheets, databases, presentation slide generators, concordancers and web page producers all have their place in the language classroom, particularly in one where the main curricular focus is task-based or project-work. The most important role of the computer in the language classroom is its use as a writing tool. It has played a significant part in the introduction of the writing process, by allowing students easily to produce multiple drafts of the same piece of work. Students with messy handwriting can now do a piece of work to be proud of, and those with poor spelling skills can, after sufficient training in using the spell check, produce a piece of writing largely free of spelling mistakes.

D.   Computer as a Data Source

Anyone who has done a search on the World Wide Web will know that there is already more information out there than an individual could process in hundred lifetimes, and the amount is growing by the second. This huge source of information is an indispensable resource for much project work, but there are serious negative implications. As an alternative to the Web, there are very many CD ROMs, e.g. encyclopaedias, that present information in a more compact, reliable and easily accessible form.

E.   Computer as Communication Facilitator

The Internet is the principal medium by which students can communicate with others at a distance. In fact, in many schools the single most popular use of computers by students in their free time is to write e-mails to their friends. Some teachers have set up joint projects with a school in another location and others encourage students to take part in discussion groups. There is no doubt that such activities are motivating for students and allow them to participate in many authentic language tasks. However, cautious teachers may wish to closely supervise their students' messages.

Computer in Distance Learning

In recent years, educators have witnessed the rapid development of computer networks, dramatic improvements in the processing power of personal computers, and striking advances in magnetic storage technology. These developments have made the computer a dynamic force in distance education, providing a new and interactive means of overcoming time and distance to reach learners.

Computer applications for distance education fall into four broad categories:

1. Computer Assisted Instruction (CAI)
CAI uses the computer as a self-contained teaching machine to present discrete lessons to achieve specific but limited educational objectives. There are several CAI modes, including: drill and practice, tutorial, simulations and games, and problem-solving.

2. Computer Managed Instruction (CMI)
CMI uses the computer's branching, storage, and retrieval capabilities to organize instruction and track student records and progress. The instruction need not be delivered via computer, although often CAI (the instructional component) is combined with CMI.

3. Computer Mediated Communication (CMC)
CMC describes computer applications that facilitate communication. Examples include electronic mail, computer conferencing, and electronic bulletin boards.

4. Computer-Based Multimedia
Computer-based Multimedia, HyperCard, hypermedia, and a still-developing generation of powerful, sophisticated, and flexible computing tools have gained the attention of distance educators in recent years. The goal of computer-based multimedia is to integrate various voice, video, and computer technologies into a single, easily accessible delivery system.

Computer in Higher Education

The dramatic increase in the use of computer-aided instruction in higher education has come to the point that the use of a computer for a range of learning tasks is now a part of a student's basic learning toolkit, as much as taking notes or reading texts.

1.   Computer in Medical Education
Information technology is an increasingly important tool for accessing and managing medical information—both patient specific and more general scientific knowledge. Medical educators are aware of the need for all medical students to learn to use information technology effectively. Computers also can play a direct role in the education process; students may interact with educational computer programs to

acquire factual information and to learn and practice problem-solving techniques. In addition, practicing physicians may use computers to expand and reinforce their professional skills throughout their careers. Computer Based Education systems have the potential to help students to master subject matter and to develop problem-solving skills. Properly integrated into the medical school curriculum and into the information systems that serve health care institutions and the greater medical community, computer-based teaching can become part of a comprehensive system for lifelong education. The challenge to researchers in computer-based teaching is to develop this potential. The barriers to success are both technical and practical. To overcome them, we require both dedication of support and resources within institutions and a commitment to cooperation among institutions.

2.   Computers in Engineering Education

The use of computers for simulation and modelling is already being added to science, analysis, and experimentation as a fourth basic component of engineering education. This inclusion is driven by engineering practice where computer use is pervasive for many purposes, including the use of complex design programs which have been created by specialists. The fact that such designers can support a large clientele by means of computer produced designs raises the question of how the larger number of future engineers, the users of such programs, should be educated. The educational challenge is to broadly educate these engineers in several aspects of engineering and computing without sacrificing the development of physical intuition and design judgment, which are the essence of engineering.

3.   Data Mining

Data mining, the extraction of hidden predictive information from large databases, is a powerful new technology with great potential to help companies focus on the most important information in their data warehouses. Higher education institutions are the nuclei of research and future development acting in a competitive environment, with the prerequisite mission to generate, accumulate and share knowledge. The chain of generating knowledge inside and among external organizations (such as companies, other universities, partners, community) is considered essential to reduce the limitations of internal resources and could be plainly improved with the use of data mining technologies. Data mining has proven to be in the recent years a pioneering field of research and investigation that faces a large variety of techniques applied in a multitude of areas, both in business and higher education, relating interdisciplinary studies and development and covering a large variety of practice. Universities require an important amount of significant knowledge mined from its past and current data sets using special methods and processes. The ways in which information and knowledge are represented and delivered to the university managers are in a continuous transformation due to the involvement of the information and communication technologies in all the academic processes. Higher education institutions have long been interested in predicting the paths of students and alumni, thus identifying which students will join particular course programs, and which students will require assistance in order to graduate.

Another important preoccupation is the academic failure among students which has long fuelled a large number of debates. Researchers attempted to classify students into different clusters with dissimilar risks in exam failure, but also to detect with realistic accuracy what and how much the students know, in order to deduce specific learning gaps. The distance and on-line education, together with the intelligent tutoring systems and their capability to register its exchanges with students present various feasible information sources for the data mining processes. Studies based on collecting and interpreting the information from several courses could possibly assist teachers and students in the web-based learning setting.

4. Cloud Computing

Cloud computing is the use of computing resources (hardware and software) that are delivered as a service over a network (typically the Internet). The name comes from the use of a cloud-shaped symbol as an abstraction for the complex infrastructure it contains in system diagrams. Cloud computing entrusts remote services with a user's data, software and computation.

Cloud computing for distributed university campus is the new trend. Public cloud computing will deliver benefits beyond the major universities. Its advantages may be even more pronounced in small colleges that have not yet achieved high levels of computerization, or do not have and have trouble recruiting people with adequate IT skills, or those worried about their ability to secure and protect data. By contracting with a cloud service provider (perhaps another, larger university), that small college can adopt state-of-the-art applications and services, enabling the college to skip a whole generation of academic computing, thereby bypassing many of the costly and debilitating challenges.

5. Mobile Computing

In recent years universities have made significant investments in corporate technology systems to support various aspects of students' studies and learning. These include gateways and learning management systems, all of which work on the assumption of attracting or pulling students into the online environment of the university. On the other hand, students come increasingly equipped with mobile devices, most notably mobile phones, which allow quick and easy communication and information sharing. These devices are an emerging phenomenon of significance for online teaching and learning as they represent opportunities for technology solutions where students can be primed and supported in novel ways in their university education. The challenge is one of achieving a balanced and sustainable use of corporate systems designed to pull students into the learning environment, and mobile technology solutions which can push information out to students, so that each adds value to and complements the other.

6. Soft Computing

Soft computing is a new name that covers different algorithms that have all something in common; they have origins in nature, which is the reason that we call them all also as natural algorithms. It covers the following disciplines: neural networks, evolutionary algorithms and fuzzy logic. First, learning automata as special type of stochastic automata are described, because they can be used to explain basic features of neural networks. Neural networks are followed by describing different models of neurons, topologies and learning algorithms. The areas of their use are given together with several examples. Evolutionary algorithms are following the theory of Darwin. We show the basic ideas of genetic algorithms, genetic programming, evolutionary strategies and evolutionary programming. The area of their exploitation is shown through examples. Fuzzy logic is introduced next, together with fuzzy decisions, fuzzy control and fuzzy inference. Finally, some joint areas are given, that combine the above disciplines.

7.   Video Conferencing

Video conferencing has great potential for learning in Higher Education. The potential lies in creating greater opportunity for dialogue which facilitates more effective learning than working in isolation. Dialogue may be between tutors and learners or amongst learners. However, the success of video conferencing may well be dependent on factors other than the technology. These factors range from Institutional issues, to cost, to student and tutors attitude to the technology. It is also highly dependent on the teaching methods adopted. There are many unanswered questions from an educational and psychological perspective. The technology is in a transitional state and many may feel it is currently unsuitable for education. This makes video conferencing highly challenging and exciting to some and a nightmare to others. Like the telephone in the past, we as users must learn how to make best use of video conferencing. It may well be the next mode of communication to be universally accepted.

The important advantages are:

1. Effective support from remote learners, experts, professionals and researchers
2. Cost effectiveness
3. Flexibility in system
4. Saving of time and Reduction in travel
5. Familiar instruction mode
6. Easy scheduling adjustment
7. Multi-vocational access control
8. Increased knowledge transfer
9. No geographical restraint
10. Immediate feed back

Computer in Special Education

Researchers and teachers have found that technological innovations can help the playing field for special needs students and enable these students to succeed in the regular classroom.

Technology for students with special needs is defined as "any item, piece of equipment, or product system, whether acquired commercially off the shelf, modified, or customized, that is used to increase, maintain, or improve functional capabilities of individuals with disabilities." This broad definition encompasses a wide variety of both high-end and low-end technologies that have proven to be useful for improving educational options for students with disabilities. The following sections describe how various applications of computer technology can help meet the individual needs of students with disabilities and enable them to function effectively in the school setting.

1. Students with Mild Learning and Behavioural Disorders

Most children with mild learning disabilities spend at least some portion of the school day in the regular classroom, even though many of these students find it difficult to keep up with their nondisabled peers and their teachers often find it difficult to spend significant amounts of time providing them with individual attention. Technology has proven to be an effective method of giving such students opportunities to engage in basic drill and practice, simulations, exploratory, or communication activities that are matched to their individual needs and abilities.

A. Word Processing Software

The attributes of word processing that lead to its effectiveness as a learning tool for children with special needs are generally the same attributes that make it effective for children in general. The word processor frees students from the more tedious duties related to the editing process, enabling them to spend more time on the content of their written products. These benefits are significant for the many students with mild learning disorders related to deficits in written language skills who often need to spend a significant amount of time rewriting a passage to communicate an idea clearly.

B. Word Prediction Software

With the help of word prediction software, students with mild learning disabilities are better able to compete academically in regular classroom settings. This software, when used in conjunction with traditional word processing programs, reduces the number of keystrokes that are required to type words and provides assistance with spelling for students of various ability levels.

C. Communication Technologies

The ability to collaborate on meaningful projects is especially beneficial for students with learning disabilities because they often have both academic and social needs to be addressed. Collaborative efforts can foster academic learning among these students by providing more "knowledge construction" activities, such as generating new ideas and building on the thoughts of others as a topic is analyzed, and by actively engaging them in the learning process. Technology facilitates the students' ability to make personal connections with others and provides opportunities to focus on writing skills within a context that they value, without fear of being stigmatized.

D. Hyperlinks and Multimedia Environments

Hyperlinks are helpful for all students, but they can be especially helpful for students with mild learning disabilities. If a student is reading a book and encounters a reference to another work then he would enhance understanding of the content. Students with mild learning disabilities often demonstrate higher-level performance and attention to detail working on multimedia projects than they normally exhibit. Research demonstrates that learning environments that incorporate dynamic images and sound are especially helpful for students who have limited background knowledge in a subject, which is often the case for students with learning disabilities.

2. Students with Speech and Language Disorders

Two general types of communication disorders qualify a student for special education services: speech disorders and language disorders. A speech disorder occurs when the speaker's articulation, voice quality, or fluency patterns impair the listener's ability to understand the intent of the speaker. A language disorder occurs when either the sender or the receiver of the message is unable to use the sounds, signs, or rules of the communication language.

Fortunately, advances in computer technology have led to the creation of specialized devices—called augmentative and alternative communication (AAC) devices—that help make it possible for individuals with no speech, or individuals with poor speech, to overcome their communication problems. Augmentative devices are designed to support or enhance the speaking capability of a person. Alternative devices, on the other hand, replace speech as a means of communication. AAC systems can be extremely powerful tools enabling some students with severe communication disorders to participate in instructional activities alongside their non-disabled peers.

3. Students with Hearing Impairments

Telecommunication Device for the Deaf (TDD) devices that assist students with severe hearing impairments have become commonplace in special education. TDDs allow users to use a keyboard to type and receive messages over the phone lines; captioning refers to the addition of text to a visual display, where the words that are spoken are seen as text. Although TDDs are devices that primarily enhance the lives of students with hearing impairments outside of school, captioning has been found to be especially helpful in promoting the inclusion of students with hearing loss in the regular classroom environment. For example, video captioning and captioned educational programs have proven to be very helpful in motivating students with hearing disabilities to learn to read. Because the nature of a hearing loss tends to cause language and communication problems, particularly in understanding situations, conversations, and written materials, studies indicate that the average reading levels of students who are deaf are considerably lower than the levels of their hearing peers of similar intellectual ability.

4. Students with Visual Impairments

Computer-based application such as optical character recognition (OCR) technology, can scan and read text aloud, allowing individuals with visual impairments greater access to all types of print materials and enabling them to read the materials independently. OCR software is now available for most computers and scanners, and several dedicated portable devices have also been developed, making them more user-friendly. The current OCR technology cannot be read handwritten materials accurately, this barrier will likely fall by the wayside in the very near future. Finally, advances in computer technology have made even the use of Braille more useful. A number of software applications have been developed that combine Braille with computer technology, such as Braille note takers, small, portable devices that can store Braille characters and read text aloud—to assist students with visual impairments in the classroom.

A. Computer Screen Magnification

Most computers sold today allow for the magnification of the screen through the use of special software. Typically, the user can select a portion of the screen and then enlarge that section up to 16 times the original size. Although the user is somewhat inconvenienced by having to view a smaller portion of the original screen as the magnification increases, this technology makes it possible for students with visual impairments to use computers in ways similar to their non-disabled peers.

B. Descriptive Video Services (DVS):

DVS technology inserts a narrative verbal description of visual elements—such as sets and costumes, characters' physical descriptions, and facial expressions—into pauses in a program's dialogue. DVS technologies help students by providing them with access to information, and through the increased opportunities to discuss programs and movies that are part of the popular culture, by providing them with opportunities for increased socialization and knowledge building.

C. Screen Readers

Screen reader software represents what is known as a text-to-speech application, which analyzes letters, words, and sentences and converts them into synthetic or digital speech. Today, text-to-speech software is common in many software packages, including many word processing and educational software programs in math, reading, and spelling. With synthetic speech, the computer reads text passages, analyzes the phonetic structure of words, and attempts to reconstruct the words by putting together a string of synthetic phonemes that are then "spoken" by the computer.

D. Optical Character Recognition (OCR)

OCR technology enables blind students to place books or other print materials on a scanner and have the text interpreted and read using synthetic or digital speech. Today, there are portable stand-alone OCR devices and devices that can attach to other computers and scanners.

E. Braille Note takers

Braille note takers are small, portable devices that enable students to enter and store Braille characters in the form of words and sentences. The note takers use the same six keys found on a traditional Braille writer used for making a paper copy of Braille. However, most notetakers allow users to review what they have written by listening to the text-to-speech function of the device. In addition, software translators allow the Braille to be converted into text. The stored files can then be used with a standard word processor or a screen reader. To get a hard copy of the information that was entered, the user can connect the notetaker directly to a standard printer for text output or a Braille printer for Braille output. Similarly, a paperless Braille display can be attached to a computer or a personal notetaker that can display up to 80 characters simultaneously. Devices such as the Braille notetaker that combine Braille with computer technology have made Braille much more useful than it was in the past.

5. Students with Severe Physical Disabilities

A number of alternative input devices can be connected to a standard computer to assist or replace the use of a traditional keyboard, which is often the greatest barrier to computer use for students with physical disabilities. Adaptive keyboards, infrared sensors, and voice recognition systems, described in Box, all have proven to be highly effective in helping students with severe physical disabilities use computers to participate in many educational activities that would not be available to them through other means.

6. Students with Mental Retardation

Computer technology offers promising new approaches to reducing the dependence of people with mental retardation on others. The results of the use of computer technology based on multimedia palmtop computer program for use in supporting individuals with mental retardation to more independently complete community-referenced vocational skills is great. Researchers in this field identified computer system requirements that would be required to accommodate the needs of people with mental retardation, and then developed and tested a "proof-of-concept" prototype of the Visual Assistant system. Results demonstrated that support for using a multimedia training program on a palmtop PC to enhance self-direction of adults with mental retardation in performing community-based vocational tasks is a must. Use of the Visual Assistant prototype helps in improved task accuracy and decreased use of external prompts from a support person on two different vocational tasks. This is a clear implication for use of palmtop and handheld PC technology to increase the independence and self-determination of individuals with mental retardation and other developmental disabilities is considered.

7. Education of Talented and Gifted Children

Gifted and talented children are those identified by professionally qualified persons who by virtue of outstanding abilities are capable of high performance. These are children who require differentiated educational programs and/or services beyond those normally provided by the regular school program in order to realize their contribution to self and society.

Measures of ability, aptitude, and intelligence are designed to indicate a person's potential to learn to solve complex problems, accomplish complex tasks, and function in other cognitively challenging arenas. A high level of ability, aptitude, or intelligence in an area indicates good potential to achieve a high level of expertise within the area. An increasing level of expertise in an area means an increasing level of knowledge and skills to solve problems within the area. One can get better at problem solving with a specific area by studying within that area. In addition, some aspects of problem solving knowledge and skill transfer among domains. That is, it is helpful both to gain domain-specific problem-solving knowledge and skills, and it is also helpful to work across disciplines and gain domain independent problem-solving knowledge and skills. ICT provides tools (as well as ways of thinking) that cut across many disciplines. Thus, ICT fits in well with many talented and gifted students who are aiming at both breadth and depth in education.

Computer in Educational Research

Research is required in any field to come up with new theories or modify, accept, or nullify the existing theory. From time immemorial it has been observed that so many discoveries and inventions took place through research and world has got so many new theories which help human being to solve his problems. Research purifies human life. It improves its quality. It is a search for knowledge. It shows how to Solve any problem scientifically. It is a careful enquiry through search for any kind of Knowledge. It is a journey from known to unknown. It is a systematic effort to gain new knowledge in any kind of discipline. When it seeks a solution of any educational problem it leads to educational research.

The various steps involved in the research process and the use of computer in each stage can be summarised as follows;

1. Identifying the Gap in Knowledge

Educational research is the systematic collation and analysis of information to help improve the quality of the learning process. Educational research draws on a mix of theoretical and empirical work from a range of disciplines but is heavily influenced by social science paradigms. Whilst the growth of theoretical knowledge continues to be important, much educational research in educational sector is directed towards addressing practical or practice-based problems, assessment and factors affecting learning environments. The success of the research lies in the sound knowledge of researcher about the problem and the knowledge gap may lead to faulty conclusions. Although we have traditional sources of knowledge, we cannot deny the power and sufficiency of cyber resources. So in identifying the knowledge gap and overcoming the knowledge gap, the researcher has to utilize computer technology.

2. Identifying the Antecedent

On the basis of experience, observation and a review of related literature only, a researcher realises that the reason for the problems identified. For spotting out the problems and for the identification of causes, one has to review sufficient related literature. The latest reviews are available in the internet. Before the journal reach in the library, one can access the same electronically. So computer technology plays a significant role in identifying the exact antecedents based upon a sound review.

3. Stating the Goals and Formulating Hypotheses

The researcher now states the goals of the study like to ascertain the relationship of variable or differences between variables. In this stage, the researcher states the goals according to his sound platform of the knowledge and some initial calculations. In this stage, the researcher makes use of computer technology.

4. Collecting Relevant Information

The researcher uses appropriate tools and techniques to measure anxiety and academic performance of students, selects a sample from the population and collects data from them. Here in collection of data, most researchers use email services to distant and rare population.

5. Testing the Hypotheses

Here the researcher uses appropriate statistical techniques to verify and test the hypotheses of the study. Here the SPSS package gives much easiness and flexibility.

6. Interpreting the Findings

Nowadays, it is very easy for the researcher to find out even the minute using SPSS. It is less-time consuming and accurate when compared to manual calculations.

7. Comparing the Findings with Prior researchers' Findings

At this step, the researcher tries to find out whether his conclusions match those of the prior researches or not. If not, then the researcher attempts to find out why conclusions do not match with other researches by analysing prior studies further. Here a researcher can make use of computer technology.

8. Preparation of Thesis

It is very important for a researcher to know how to use a computer for accessing information and writing the thesis. They should how the software can help them to do tasks like fill in citations, maintain a consistent style, create a Table of Contents, and import work done on other software. Conventions are the rules that we need to follow in writing regarding citations, bibliographies, style, page setup, punctuation, spelling, figures and tables, and the presentation of graphics. Computer programs such as End Note are available so that one may like to find out which systems of conventions they employ and choose accordingly. Programs such as Word for Windows include templates for dissertations (and other kinds of writing); these help one to maintain a consistent use of conventions throughout your thesis.

Computer in Educational Administration

Initially, the establishment of computers in schools, colleges, universities and research institutes in India was for educational and research purposes. But gradually the management and policy makers realised the potentiality of computers in the area of educational administration, namely, admission, examination, accounting, inventory management, library materials management, student record keeping, etc. Computers are well suited for information processing tasks because of their speed, accuracy, and ability to store large data in an accessible form. As school systems have grown in size and in the scope of their activities, computer technology has provided mechanism for administrators to keep abreast of increasing demands for current and documented information. The following are some of the areas where computers can be used for effective educational administration.

1. Computer Based General Administration

Office automation facilitates the basic functions of an office as an information processing centre. The functions of office personnel at the lowest information handling level (clerical level) namely Office Automation System (OAS), involve: (a)

Collection of information (b) Information processing (c) Information storing and (d) Information retrieval.

2. Computer Based Payroll and Financial Accounting

Computers are used widely for preparation and maintenance of payrolls system. Initially, large business establishments were using payroll system. It has the potential in terms of time saving, accuracy, legibility, data storage, record check, and amenable for further data analysis, comparative statements, task calculations, and preparation of summary reports. These activities influenced even smaller establishments like secondary schools to use the computer for maintenance of payroll system. Currently, the salary payments to teachers, and other staff of the schools are paid through banks. Through computer payroll system the school can prepare the summary statements of the net pay of its staff and the same can be shared with the banks electronically or hard copy to facilitate the bankers to pay the salary due.

3. Computer Based Administration of Student Data

The major applications of computers which have direct impact on the students are course schedules, attendance, and academic performance. Once the student admission process is completed, the school administration needs to maintain time-tables on completion schedules of syllabus; conducting unit tests, term-end examinations, and final examinations; and announcement of results. Similarly, the teachers have to be assigned the individual classes and subjects that they should cover. This also helps the administration to assess the teacher load. Generation of course schedules and their implementation through computers will certainly improve the control and management of academic calendar.

Attendance of students is a major concern to school administrators and teachers. The rules of schools also stipulate minimum attendance as a prerequisite for appearing examination and clearing a course. This has resulted in the establishment of elaborate attendance systems that have sought to monitor accurately the daily attendance of students. As compared to manual attendance maintenance system, a computerised system will be able to meet the objectives in a better and more effective way.

Computers are being used widely in the process of examination results. In addition, currently, there is a lot of competition for certain courses like engineering, medical, management, computer science etc. Similarly a number of reputed schools/colleges are also facing the problem of admission process, due to large number of students seeking admission and the seat availability is limited. These schools or colleges are conducting entrance examinations to screen the applications for admission to competitive courses. Computerisation of entrance examination process facilitates greatly to announce the ranks obtained by students and final admission of students to various courses in shortest possible time. This also helps the students to work out their own alternative career choices depending on the ranks obtained by students, course-wise and college-wise seats available, and the demand for individual courses and colleges.

4. Computer Based Inventory Management

Schools are required to maintain all supplies and equipment. The physical inventory should be taken by school periodically in agreement of accounts with records. The inventory list should identify each item by date of purchase, cost, location, item control number, and date of last inventory. The inventory system should facilitate adding new equipment and furniture to the master file, removing old or obsolete equipment, and recording the transfer of items. By having an effective inventory system, a school can (a) enhance the functioning of school, (b) aid cost accounting and development of budget, and (c) avoidance of excessive stocks and shortage of stocks. Also, the effective control of inventory is achieved by maintaining appropriate levels of inventory and minimising the inventory losses.

5. Computer Based Personnel Records Maintenance

Every school has to develop a personnel information system for the following purposes: (a) to store personnel details (like name, address, telephone number, date of birth, educational qualifications and experience, salary, health data etc.) of individual employees for reference. (b) To provide a basis for decision-making in every area of personnel work like recruitment and selection, termination and redundancy, education and training, pay, administration, health etc.

Personnel records can be maintained manually. However, the advent of micro-computers has increased the process of computerisation even in personnel records maintenance. The maintenance of personnel records on each employees of a school should include information on: 1. the application form giving personal particulars 2. Interview and test record 3. Job history including transfers, promotions, and changes in occupation 4. Pay details 5. Education and training record 6. Details of performance assessment and appraisal 7. Absence, accident, medical and disciplinary records with details of formal warnings and suspensions.

6. Computer Based Library Systems

Applications of computers in school libraries can be classified into: (a) library automation, (b) information storage and retrieval, and (c) library networks. The term 'library automation' refers to computerisation of manual library activities. Library automation functions include book ordering system, cataloguing, circulation control, and periodicals control systems.

The developments in the information technology particularly in the area of on-line storage and retrieval of large database have made great impact on libraries (online storage and retrieval of bibliographical and other database information). A bibliographical database must be non-redundant and multi-usable. Computerisation of the library database has these special features. Also, library database enables the users to have a centralised control of data.

The promotion of databases in India especially by National Informatics Centre (NIC) has influenced libraries to establish a computer network to share bibliographic information. The advent of internet has further strengthened the library information network in India. A number of networks are started functioning and many more are in the pipeline. For example, DELNET, a Delhi based network connects major libraries located in universities and research institutes in Delhi. Each participating institute prepares computerised bibliographic information and connects it to the network. The user can find out the books available of his interest and their location. They can also get the books on loan through participating institutes. This avoids the duplication of buying expensive books by institutions and saves a lot of money.

Social Networking as an Educational Tool

Social networking plays an integral role in the lives of teenagers. Social networking is not just a vile place filled with child predators, Cyber bullying, and opportunities to turn teenagers into unwilling criminals; it also provides invaluable benefits, including opportunities for self-reflection, identity exploration and formation, and social and academic support. Social networking creates opportunities for teachers to seize and use this underutilized educational tool to enrich the academic lives of their students.

Social networking among adolescents is not just a fad; it is part of their culture. While social networking can expose teens to danger, they are exposed to the same dangers in real life as well. A parent or teacher cannot expect a teen to abandon the internet and be able to thrive in modern society as computers, technology, the internet, and social networking is utilized in all aspects of modern life, even in the workplace. This is why social networking should be included as a valuable tool to enhance the classroom but should also be utilized as an opportunity to teach students the skills that ensure safe and enriching use of social media.

In the field of education, social-networking sites offer a student the opportunity to connect with other students, educators, administrators, alumni, both within and outside his current institution. Scholars praise social-networking tools for their capability to attract, motivate and engage students in meaningful communicative practice, content exchange, and collaboration.

The social networking is easy and quick in term of accessing accessibility, reviewing, updating, and editing learning material needs anytime and anywhere. In addition, it allows for option to select learning materials from large quantity of courses offered online which the learner needs and it also makes easier distribution of courses material. The social networking helps to reduce stress and increase satisfaction among students. It allows each student (slow or quick) to study at their own pace and speed (self-pacing). Furthermore, it is easy to join bulletin board discussion any time, or visiting classmates and instructors remotely in chat room. It can provide stronger understanding and increase retention on the subject , due to using many elements which exist under e-learning, e.g. multimedia, quizzes, interaction ... etc and the ability too retry training and over in order to understand. The social networking allows access to courses available in their sites, allowing the learner to follow-up online at any time it deems appropriate, and overcome the limitations of space and time in the educational process. As a result, it helps resolve timetable conflicts.

There are some benefits and obstacles that one faces in using social networking as educational tool. Privacy, real friendship, time consumption and miscommunication are the most important challenges facing education through the social networking. On the other hand, flexibility, repeatable and convenience and accessibility have a vital influence in the use of social networking in education.

Computer as Non-print and Print Media of Education

The role of media is central to the success of distance education. Since most of the time learners are at a distance (i.e. quasi-permanent separation of learner from the teacher) from their teachers the content is delivered using different media. Here the predominant medium is normally the printed text. However, printed text does not replace teachers altogether. But the invention of the printed text did lead to the re-organisation of teaching and opening of access to education. The emergence of the print medium and the subsequent introduction of postal system led to open up education for those, who could not attend regular classes. Thus, correspondence education came into existence and it continued for long. However, over time the use of 'non-print' media became increasingly popular in distance education.

The emergence of microcomputer has heralded a new era in the use of computers in education. Microcomputers allow users to process information locally with the potentiality to even connect to remote computers through networks. Microcomputers can he used for word processing, maintaining a database, desk-top publishing, running computer-assisted learning packages, sending communication through e-mail, etc. From the educational use view point of computer media, the other related developments are availability of Graphical User Interface (user friendly screens), higher storage capacity (CD ROMs), network ability of computers (Computer Mediated Communication) and the Internet.

In distance education, the computer is being considered a more open and flexible delivery media that can be adapted to varying individual needs in terms of time, place, pace and choice of content. The computer-based media in distance education are primarily available in three modes - Independent, Interactive and

Communication. In the independent mode, it is the Computer and its various facilities that are put to use by the leaner to use word-processing software, to compute data using a spreadsheet or to develop a database. In a way the learner works on a computer system. Whereas In the interactive mode, the learner makes use of a pre-programmed learning package (e.g. Computer-Aided Instruction, Computer managed learning) to learn the skills, concepts and processes. The learning package provides opportunity for interaction and feedback for enhanced learning. The third role is communication, where the learner communicates with another learner or teacher using the computer to learn cooperatively.

UNIT – VII

INSTRUCTIONAL METHODS

Instructional Methods

Every method a teacher uses has advantages, disadvantages and requires some preliminary preparation. So what else is new? Three broad categories of instructional methods are teacher talk, student talk, and student-teacher interactive talk. Often a particular method will naturally flow into another, all within the same lesson. Which instructional method is "right" for a particular lesson depends on many things and among them are the age and developmental level of the students, what the students already know, and what they need to know to succeed with the lesson, the subject-matter content, the objective of the lesson, the available people, time, space and material resources, and the physical setting. A difficult problem is to select an instructional method that best fits one's particular teaching style and the lesson-situation. There is no one "right" method for teaching a particular lesson, but there are some criteria that pertain to each that can help a teacher make the best decision possible.

Programmed Instruction

Programmed instruction is the name of the technology invented by the behaviorist B.F. Skinner to improve teaching. It is based on his theory of verbal behavior as a means to accelerate and increase conventional educational learning. It typically consists of self-teaching with the aid of a specialized textbook or teaching machine that presents material structured in a logical and empirically developed sequence or sequences. Programmed instruction may be presented by a teacher as well, and it has been argued that the principles of programmed instruction can improve classic lectures and textbooks. Programmed instruction allows students to progress through a unit of study at their own rate, checking their own answers and advancing only after answering correctly. In one simplified form of PI, after each step, they are presented with a question to test their comprehension, then are immediately shown the correct answer or given additional information. However the objective of the instructional programming is to present the material in very small increments. The more sophisticated forms of programmed instruction may have the questions or tasks programmed well enough that the presentation and test model—an extrapolation from traditional and classical instruction—is not necessarily utilized.

Programmed instruction is a method of presenting new subject matters to students in a graded sequence of controlled steps. Students work through the programmed material by themselves at their own speed and after each step test their comprehension by answering an examination question or filling in a diagram. They are then immediately shown the correct answer or given additional information. Computers and other types of teaching machines are often used to present the material, although books may also be used.

Personalized System of Instruction

The Personalized System of Instruction is an approach to classroom instruction designed to change the role of teacher from agent of information to the engineer or manager of student learning. Its workability has been instruction. PSI was originally designed as a classroom-based method of instruction with the intention of improving student achievement and, at the same time, replacing the long tradition of punishment in education with the use of positive consequences for learning. The Personalized System of Instruction is a mastery learning model which seeks to promote mastery of a pre-specified set of objectives from each learner in a course. Students work through a series of self-paced modules

The Personalized System of Instruction fits into several paradigms, but is most closely aligned with direct instruction. It fits with direct instruction by requiring student to work on course modules independently. It fits slightly with social constructivism by also requiring students to meet weekly in peer teams with a proctor to answer questions and take a quiz on the content studied. Students do not engage in considerable team work as most social constructivist models advocate, rather, they only correct one another's responses to proctor-led questions.

Objectives of PSI

- To establish better personal-social relationship in the educational process.
- To provide frequent reinforcement to the learners.
- To provide increased frequency and quality of feedback to the designers with the consequent benefit of a basis for meaningful revision in programme-content structures and instructional procedures.
- To reduce the reliance of the lecture for presentation or critical information by employing different devices in the instructional procedures
- To evaluate the student's performance as compared with other students.

Computer Assisted Instruction (CAI)

A self-learning technique, usually offline/online, involving interaction of the student with programmed instructional materials. Computer-assisted instruction (CAI) is an interactive instructional technique whereby a computer is used to present the instructional material and monitor the learning that takes place. CAI uses a combination of text, graphics, sound and video in enhancing the learning process. The computer has many purposes in the classroom, and it can be utilized to help a student in all areas of the curriculum. CAI refers to the use of the computer as a tool to facilitate and improve instruction. CAI programs use tutorials, drill and practice, simulation, and problem solving approaches to present topics, and they test the student's understanding.

Types of Computer Assisted Instruction

1. Drill-and-practice Drill and practice provide opportunities to students to repeatedly practice the skills that have previously been presented and that further practice is necessary for mastery.

2. Tutorial Tutorial activity includes both the presentation of information and its extension into different forms of work, including drill and practice, games and simulation.

3. Games Game software often creates a contest to achieve the highest score and either beat others or beat the computer.

4. Simulation Simulation software can provide an approximation of reality that does not require the expense of real life or its risks.

5. Discovery Discovery approach provides a large database of information specific to a course or content area and challenges the learner to analyze, compare, infer and evaluate based on their explorations of the data.

6. Problem Solving This approach helps children develop specific problem solving skills and strategies.

Advantages of CAI
• one-to-one interaction
• great motivator
• freedom to experiment with different options
• instantaneous response/immediate feedback to the answers elicited
• Self pacing - allow students to proceed at their own pace
• Helps teacher can devote more time to individual students
• Privacy helps the shy and slow learner to learns
• Individual attention
• learn more and more rapidly
• multimedia helps to understand difficult concepts through multi sensory approach
• self directed learning – students can decide when, where, and what to learn

Limitations of CAI

• may feel overwhelmed by the information and resources available
• over use of multimedia may divert the attention from the content
• learning becomes too mechanical
• non availability of good CAI packages
• lack of infrastructure

Teaching Method

A teaching method comprises the principles and methods used for instruction. Commonly used teaching methods may include class participation, demonstration, recitation, memorization, or combinations of these. The choice of teaching method or methods to be used depends largely on the information or skill that is being taught, and it may also be influenced by the aptitude and enthusiasm of the students.

Lecture Method

Often the cornerstone of university teaching, a lecture can be an effective method for communicating theories, ideas, and facts to students. Typically a structured presentation, a lecture should be designed to include certain procedures in order to be effective–procedures that research and expert lecturers have identified as essential to assist student learning. Perhaps you are not totally satisfied with your lecturing skills? Or not satisfied with your students' learning from the lectures you present? By following the guidelines for lecture design that are based on learning theory, you will use your lecture preparation time most efficiently. The basic purpose of lecturing is the dissemination of information. As an expert in your field, you identify important information for the learner and transmit this knowledge in the lecture. The lecture method is recommended for high consensus disciplines–those in which there is agreement on the fundamental principles and procedures, such as maths and the natural sciences.

Advantages/Disadvantages

The following are the **basic advantages** of the lecture method:
- It provides an economical and efficient method for delivering substantial amounts of information to large numbers of student.
- It affords a necessary framework or overview for subsequent learning, e.g., reading assignments, small group activities, discussion.
- It offers current information (more up to date than most texts) from many sources.
- It provides a summary or synthesis of information from different sources.
- It creates interest in a subject as lecturers transmit enthusiasm about their discipline.

There are **disadvantages** to using the lecture method as a primary teaching method. An effective lecture requires both extensive research and preparation and effective delivery skills to maintain students' attention and motivation. In addition, the lecture has other drawbacks:
- It does not afford the instructor with ways to provide students with individual feedback.
- It is difficult to adapt to individual learning differences.
- It may fail to promote active learning unless other teaching strategies, such as questioning and problem-solving activities, are incorporated into the lecture.
- It does not promote independent learning.

Demonstration Method

Demonstration involves showing by reason or proof, explaining or making clear by use of examples or experiments. Put more simply, demonstration means to clearly show. In teaching through demonstration, students are set up to potentially conceptualize class material more effectively as shown in a study which specifically focuses on chemistry demonstrations presented by teachers. Demonstrations often occur when students have a hard time connecting theories to actual practice or when

126

students are unable to understand application of theories. Teachers not only demonstrate specific learning concepts within the classroom, they can also participate in demonstration classrooms to help improve their own teaching strategies, which may or may not be demonstrative in nature. Although the literature is limited, studies show that the effects of demonstration classroom teachers includes a change of perspective in relating to students, more reflection in the teachers' own classroom strategies, and more personal responsibility for student learning.

Demonstration, or clearly showing (a gamut that ranges from mere pointing to more sophisticated strategies such as chemical reactions), can possibly be used in portraying ideas such as defining words. At first, simple observation and communication through pointing to an object, area, or place, like the sun, moon, or a large mountain top, occurs. Then basic definitions of words emerge. These definitions allow humans to communicate, interact, plan, and co-ordinate in ways that help us to build cities, large buildings, technology, gain knowledge and to successfully communicate with computers. Further, basic concepts centered on time, space, and mathematics are first required to demonstrate and teach probable theories that accurately describe universal phenomenon such as nature, planets, species, and the world around us.

Problem-solving Method

Problem-solving consists of using generic or *ad hoc* methods, in an orderly manner, for finding solutions to problems. Some of the problem-solving techniques developed and used in artificial intelligence, computer science, engineering, mathematics, medicine, etc. are related to mental problem-solving techniques studied in psychology. The term *problem-solving* is used in many disciplines, sometimes with different perspectives, and often with different terminologies. For instance, it is a mental process in psychology and a computerized process in computer science. Problems can also be classified into two different types (ill-defined and well-defined) from which appropriate solutions are to be made. Ill-defined problems are those that do not have clear goals, solution paths, or expected solution. Well-defined problems have specific goals, clearly defined solution paths, and clear expected solutions. These problems also allow for more initial planning than ill-defined problems. Being able to solve problems sometimes involves dealing with pragmatics (logic) and semantics (interpretation of the problem). The ability to understand what the goal of the problem is and what rules could be applied represent the key to solving the problem. Sometimes the problem requires some abstract thinking and coming up with a creative solution.

In computer science and in the part of artificial intelligence that deals with algorithms ("algorithmics"), problem solving encompasses a number of techniques known as algorithms, heuristics, root cause analysis, etc. In these disciplines, problem solving is part of a larger process that encompasses problem determination, de-duplication, analysis, diagnosis, repair, etc.

Project Method

The project method is a medium of instruction which was introduced during the 18th century into the schools of architecture and engineering in Europe when graduating students had to apply the skills and knowledge they had learned in the course of their studies to problems they had to solve as practicians of their trade, for example, designing a monument, building a steam engine.[1] In the early 20th Century, William Heard Kilpatrick[2] expanded the project method into a philosophy of education. His device is child-centred and based in progressive education. Both approaches are used by teachers worldwide to this day.[3] Unlike traditional education, proponents of the project method attempt to allow the student to solve problems with as little teacher direction as possible. The teacher is seen more as a facilitator than a delivery of knowledge and information.

Students in a project method environment should be allowed to explore and experience their environment through their senses and, in a sense, direct their own learning by their individual interests. Very little is taught from textbooks and the emphasis is on experiential learning, rather than rote and memorization. A project method classroom focuses on democracy and collaboration to solve "purposeful" problems.

Scientific Method

Scientific Method is a pedagogical approach used in undergraduate science classrooms whereby teaching and learning is approached with the same rigor as science itself. According to a 2004 Policy Forum in *Science* magazine, "scientific teaching involves active learning strategies to engage students in the process of science and teaching methods that have been systematically tested and shown to reach diverse students."

Three major tenets of scientific teaching:

- **Active learning**: A process in which students are actively engaged in learning. It may include inquiry-based learning, cooperative learning, or student-centered learning.
- **Assessment**: Tools for measuring progress toward and achievement of the learning goals.
- **Diversity**: The breadth of differences that make each student unique, each cohort of students unique, and each teaching experience unique. Diversity includes everything in the classroom: the students, the instructors, the content, the teaching methods, and the context.

These elements should underlie educational and pedagogical decisions in the classroom. The "SCALE-UP" learning environment is an example of applying the scientific teaching approach. In practice, scientific teaching employs a "backward design" approach. The instructor first decides what the students should know and be able to do (learning goals), then determines what would be evidence of student achievement of the learning goals, then designs assessments to measure this achievement. Finally, the instructor plans the learning activities, which should facilitate student learning through scientific discovery.

Inductive and Deductive Method

Two very distinct and opposing instructional approaches are inductive and deductive. Both approaches can offer certain advantages, but the biggest difference is the role of the teacher. In a deductive classroom, the teacher conducts lessons by introducing and explaining concepts to students, and then expecting students to complete tasks to practice the concepts; this approach is very teacher-centred. Conversely, inductive instruction is a much more student-centred approach and makes use of a strategy known as 'noticing'. Let's take a closer look at the differences between inductive and deductive instruction, and find out how noticing can be used in the language classroom to better facilitate student learning.

What is inductive instruction?

In contrast with the deductive method, inductive instruction makes use of student "noticing". Instead of explaining a given concept and following this explanation with examples, the teacher presents students with many examples showing how the concept is used. The intent is for students to "notice", by way of the examples, how the concept works. Using the grammar situation from above, the teacher would present the students with a variety of examples for a given concept without giving any preamble about how the concept is used. As students see how the concept is used, it is hoped that they will notice how the concept is to be used and determine the grammar rule. As a conclusion to the activity, the teacher can ask the students to explain the grammar rule as a final check that they understand the concept.

What is deductive instruction?

A deductive approach to instruction is a more teacher-centered approach. This means that the teacher gives the students a new concept, explains it, and then has the students practice using the concept. For example, when teaching a new grammar concept, the teacher will introduce the concept, explain the rules related to its use, and finally the students will practice using the concept in a variety of different ways. "The deductive method is often criticized because: a) it teaches grammar in an isolated way; b) little attention is paid to meaning; c) practice is often mechanical." This method can, however, be a viable option in certain situations; for example, when dealing with highly motivated students, teaching a particularly difficult concept, or for preparing students to write exams.

UNIT – VIII

INSTRUCTIONAL AIDS

Instructional material aids refer to devices and adaptations to materials that help facilitate an individual's learning. They include Braille displays or print magnifiers for students who are blind or visually impaired. Instructional material aids also include instructional technology that is used in the education of a person such as overhead transparencies and projectors, audiotape players, multimedia software and tools, internet technology for watching real-time activities, and computer software and hardware including computers with adaptive switches or adapted keyboards.

Instructional aids should not be confused with training media. Educators generally describe training media as any physical means that communicates an instructional message to students. For example, the instructor's voice, printed text, video cassettes, interactive computer programs, part-task trainers, flight training devices or flight simulators, and numerous other types of training devices are considered training media. Instructional aids, on the other hand, are devices that assist an instructor in the teaching-learning process. Instructional aids are not self-supporting; they are supplementary training devices. The key factor is that instructional aids support, supplement, or reinforce.

In general, the coverage of instructional aids in the first part of this chapter applies to a classroom setting with one instructor and several students. The discussion about types of instructional aids begins with the most basic aids and progresses to the more complex and expensive aids. The last segment is about new training technologies which may apply to a typical classroom environment, as well as other training environments.

Edgar Dale's Cone of Experience

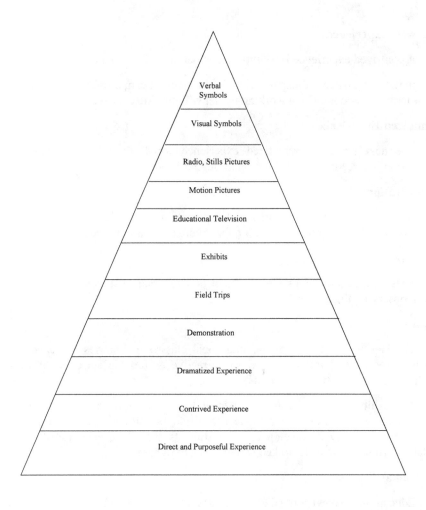

Verbal
Symbols

Visual Symbols

Radio, Stills Pictures

Motion Pictures

Educational Television

Exhibits

Field Trips

Demonstration

Dramatized Experience

Contrived Experience

Direct and Purposeful Experience

Direct Purposeful Experiences

The basic of cone represents the concrete, direct first hand experiences. In the absence of direct experiences teachers use models and mock ups.

Contrived Experiences

A contrived experience is a simplified experience through a model.

It will be difficult thing to bring in an electronic microscope or an atomic reactor in the classroom. But a working model will provide contrived experience.

Dramatized Experience

The next stage is dramatized experience which provides a situation for participation in a reconstructed situation through it is not a real experience.

Demonstrations

Demonstrations are useful in visual explanation of the phenomena. If students are involved in these activities they get a feel of creative participation.

Field trips

These are certain things which cannot be explained to students very effective without observing them in real setting.

Exhibits

The sterile appearance of the traditional classroom libraries & corridors of schools is recently giving way to warm attractive & flexible surrounding with a wealth of display materials or exhibits.

The exhibits should be the result of active participation of students and the teachers. The students take keen interest in displaying attractive material and thus their creativity ability is developed. The students should be encouraged to give regular contributions in order to keep bulletin board dynamic.

Educational Television

Educational Television (ETV) includes programmes related directly to an organized programme of formal instruction and is directed to individual viewers who come under non-formal education programme.

The educational programmes are telecast through satellite. The NCERT is producing educational TV programmes with the help of many universities in different subjects and they are telecast as UGC programme for college students.

Educational telecast tends to bring into the classroom learning experiences that locate teacher cannot arrange complicated experiments, visual excursion to far off places and current events such programmes produce good results.

Motion Pictures

Motion pictures also play an important role in the teaching learning process.

Radio & Still Pictures

Radio is one of the most important audio aids used in teaching learning activities.

Still Pictures

Generally the pictures used by the teacher in the classroom must be large or big in size. At a time all the students should see the pictures in the classroom.

Visual Symbols

The teacher should prepare proper size of the charts, posters and maps and use in the classroom. On the basis of explaining those students may get clear knowledge of them.

Verbal Symbols

The highest abstraction is through symbolic or verbal experience. A teacher uses chalk board, charts and maps to give abstract situations and students are far away from the real thing.

Verbal communication gives simple representation of thing and facts to evoke participation.

Actual objects and other specially prepared materials like slides, film strips audio and visual tapes are included in software.

The hardware can serve as a teaching aid. Hardware materials are quite dependent upon software for their services.

The software does not depend upon the hardware. On the other hand, many of the software may serve well without the help of hardware.

Projected Aids

When a projected aid is used an enlarged image of the material is projected on a screen kept all a distance from the projector. The room is either totally or partially darkened. It is more effective and attraction.

Epidiascope

Epidiascope is the combination of episcope and diascope. This device is used to project both transparent and non-transparent materials. When it is used to project non-transparent material it works and it also works when it is used to project transparent materials.

That is why it is named as epidiascope.

Transparent materials like slides, non-transparent materials such as pictures, from texts, flat pictures, photographs, postcards, student's own drawing, sketches or written materials & small objects can all be projected in magnified form on the screen.

Films

An educational film is a projected aid which contributes to the attainment of desirable educational outcomes by making an effective use of motion picture as a medium of communication.

They are useful for presenting dynamic things or visual which cannot be presented in the classroom by other means. Films have become out of data.

Educational value

- ❖ As film combines visual, motion and sound it can contribute to effective teaching and learning process.
- ❖ Film helps to motivate the students and compels attention.
- ❖ Film can reproduce certain natural phenomenon like lunar and solar eclipse etc. which are not always possible to see.
- ❖ With the help of 'Fast motion technique' and slow motion technique we can closely observe and discern the movement and process that are happening slowly or very quickly.
- ❖ It has capacity of bringing the past events and present into the classroom.

Film Strips

Film strip is a still picture visual medium. A film strip is a related sequence of transparent still pictures of images arranged in a specific order on a strip of 35mm film. It may be either single frame or double frame.

It is made of cellulose ace table sheet of 35mm width varying in a length from 2 feet to 5 feet. In case of single frame, the size of the picture is 18 X 24 mm & double frame is 24 X 36 mm.

A strip may contain 10 to 50 frames depending upon its length and type. The pictures in the frames may be drawing, photos, diagrams or the combinations of these.

It can be prepared by apply photographic techniques or by drawing pictures by hand on the film itself.

Educational values

- ❖ They are inexpensive
- ❖ They are light weight and easy to transport
- ❖ They are non-inflammable, no danger in carrying them
- ❖ They are convenient and flexible to use
- ❖ They have great power to hold attention and motivate students in teaching-learning.

Slide Projectors

It is a modern projector that provides the facility to project both filmstrip and the 2" X 2" photo slide. It is easy to operate. It is available with different kinds of illumination from small 10 watt projector for use in auditorium. This projector is designed to allow a slide carrier to be inserted.

Several automatic slide projectors are available today and slides can be loaded in a linear tray and circular tray in proper sequence. The projector can be operated and focused by remote control.

Educational values

They can be projected in a partially darkened room thus facilitating further class activities.

They may be enlarged to desired size repeatedly shown and keep the image on screen for any time. Preparation of slide is comparatively inexpensive. They are easy to handle and easy to store.

Over Head Projector

Over head projector is one of the important and versatile tools in the teaching-learning process.

Description

OHP looks like a rectangular box made up of metal sheet. Inside there is a light source and below it a concave reflector is fixed which reflects all the light rays come from the light source to the top.

A fresnel lens is fixed above to form a converging beam of light which illuminates the stage uniformly and converges to the projection lens with the help of plane mirror kept at 45° inclined the image can be reflected to fall on a screen kept behind and over the head of teacher.

Principle and Operation

In OHP, a transparent visual is placed on a horizontal stage on the top of the light source. The light passes through this transparent material and then is reflected at an angle on the screen or wall at the back side & over the head of the instructor.

EDUCATIONAL VALUES

Enlarge images

An enlarged projected image of the transparent visual is obtained in a minimum of projected distance.

Face the Students

Teacher can always face his students, observe students reaction, guide his students, control their attention and regulate the flow of information in the visual presentation.

Portable

The comparative light weight of the equipment makes it portable, simple to operate and requires only minimal servicing.

Minimize the Cost and Time

Effective visuals can be made in minimum of time and cost. Once it is made, it is permanent and need not be erased as in a chalk board.

Large group Instruction

OHP is very much useful particularly with sufficient large group.

Closed – Circuit Television (CCTV)

Closed circuit television is an internal television transmission system that distributes TV programmes like tape, both audio and video to a limited network connected by a cable system. The network may consist of school of district or several districts. The telecast cannot be received by other TV outside the network.

These must be team work among teachers with in a given discipline and co-ordination between the various teams.

EDUCATIONAL VALUES

Increase range of Instruction

CCTV enables to increase the range of instruction by one or more location beyond the classroom.

Exchange of teaching experts

It provides opportunities for exchange teachers and courses between one instruction and another linked in a circuit.

Personalized and localized Instruction

It enables institutions to present televised instruction according to their own schedules and needs.

Video – Cassette Recorder / Player

The VCR or player is helping to enhance the educational and entertainment values of TV. The instruments and the software needed for them such as video cassette are available in a variety of makes and at lower prices.

The pre-recorded cassettes on different school subjects are available now in the market and at lower prices. The school should possess a VCR or VCP and a TV. These recorded cassettes can be played for the students. The play is in colour with associated sound makes viewing dynamic and its impact on the viewers considerable.

The play can be done in one or more TVS simultaneously facilitating large audience viewing in different class rooms. New projection TV system with 6" to 10 screens & facilitates for front or back projection is available now-a-days.

Film Projector

A device for passing light through a series of still photographs recorded on film. To do this, the projection must have provision to move the film in front of a strong light source and it must be chemically start and stop the film for sometimes in front of this light.

There is a constant light source and a photo electric cell in order to produce sound. The film must move at a constant speed as to produce the sound.

Non – Projected Aids

These aids are the form of visual that cannot be projected using an equipment. They convey meaning mainly through relatively conventionalized symbols that are nearer to reality perceptually those verbal symbols.

The following are some of the non-projected aids.

Graphic Aids

Photographs

This is one of the most common type of visual aids. The photo helps the extended work to get across and idea and pass on to the audience. It is visual which has to catch the attention of the audience and pass on to them a simple message at a glance.

The audience should become aware of the event, practice or idea you want to communicate.

Pictures

Pictures are used for the expression of idea. They are more attractive and are easily understandable. Pictures should be considered as short and language of the idea presented picture are only 2-d but should be carefully planned.

This can be prepared by any teacher using simple material. They convey the expected message by combination of visual aids by suitable information effectively.

Flash Card

Flash cards are small compact cards that are flashed before a class to bring into the students mind an idea, photos or pictures may be pasted on flash cards.

They are very useful in language teaching. Flash cards are pierce of cardboard or hard paper on which letter, words phrases or a picture is drawn. They can be shown to the students at anytime. They arouse the students' curiosity. Flash cards are approximately 10" X 12" in size and 4" X 4" etc,.

Posters

Posters are basic representation striking colour of an idea of concept in an attractive form. It catches the eye and makes the view go through the message conveyed.

Good posters are simple as well as striking.

Charts

The word "chart" on the common usage means a variety of graphic etc, for the purpose of clarity it is desirable to consider charts as means of visualization with certain attributes.

It may be defined as a combination of graphics and pictorial media designed for orderly and for ideas.

Diagrams

A diagram a simplified drawing designed to show relationship primarily by means of lines and symbols. They can be truly considered as brief visual synopsis of facts to be presented.

They are indispensable in science subjects. They usually can be better used for summary and review than far instruction.

Maps

Maps are a flat representation of the earth's surface drawn into scale, partly or wholly. These are not merely fundamental for the study of geography and other subjects but are essential for a whole range of human activities. Such as interesting weather travel, current world event etc.,

Maps have innerate practical value. The language of maps are largely a language of colours and symbols standing.

Graphs

Graphs represent visual aids of depicting numerical or qualitative relationships. They are available in various forms.

Bar graphs

Circle graphs

Line graphs &

Pictorial graphs

The type we choose will largely depend on the complexity of the information we wish to present and the graph.

With the aid of graph not only the particular interpretation can be done, but also its relations with the other objects are also easily correlated. This is an important use of graphs.

Cartoons

A cartoon is a metaphoric presentation in the form of picture or a sketch. It is vigorously present and dramatize humour, caricature or exaggerating or any characteristics visual aspects.

It attracts the attention of the viewer cartoon – like poster is universal in appeal . It convey only one idea.

Comics

It is meant for conveying messages through a short story and the characters will speak the dialogue and so on.

Audio – aids

Radio

All India Radio has in its regular feature. Some programme meant for school children. The topic, data and time of broadcast of such talks are given in advance by AIR.

A school can take benefit of such talks only of it possess a good radio set and a period provided in the school time table for listening such talks.

Television

It is a powerful medium of mass communication which is also used for education.

In it the advantage of radio and film are combined.

Recorder

It helps us to record the sound in a magnetic tape and reproduce it when it is required. It consists of different parts such as volume control, speaker, recording and playback head, tap control such as play, forward, rewind, stop, pause and record and a cassette holder with motor driven spindles.

Its advantages are it is easy to operate, economical and portable.

Display Board

Blackboard

It is one of the most common visual aids in use. It is slightly abrasive writing surface made of wood, plywood, cement, slate, plastic etc. with black, green or bluish green paint on it.

It is either built into the wall or fixed and framed on the wall. It is portable chalkboards which are placed on a stand with adjustable height.

Generally white chalk sticks are used and coloured chalks are used for better illustrations. Before the beginning of teaching session the blackboard can be used for displaying the materials relevant to the topic.

Flannel board

It is otherwise called as cloth board or felt board. Two pieces of flannel will stick together when they are kept over each other and a gentle pressure is applied.

By fixing pieces of flannel (or) sand paper (or) cause materials to the back of the pictures, graphs, cartoons and other visual materials to be shown to audience it is possible to display them with this simple device. The teaching learning process can be made more interesting and simple.

Bulletin board

A bulletin board is used to deliver the message or produce action photographs, publications, drawings, posters, wall newspapers, leaflets, specimen, cuttings and illustrations are some of the items that are generally displayed. It can be used both indoor and outdoor.

It is made of soft board or khadi cloth or coconut matting and displays are pinned or bagged on it.

Magnetic Board

It is framed iron sheet having porcelain coating in black or green colour such as board can be used either to write with chalk sticks or to display pictures. Cut outs and even light objects with disc magnets or magnetic holders.

It provides the flexibility of movement of visual material. It is possible to display even a three-dimension object using magnetic holders.

Dimensional Aids

Models

Many time under practical condition the real objects are not always available. Even when they are available they might be too big or too complex and too cumbersome to handle in the teaching learning situation. The models are simulation of real objects.

Specimens

A specimen is a small piece, part or sample representation of the real objects or materials. They give an appeal the several senses, activate them arouse their interest and to bring their involvement. Specimens are mostly used in teaching of science subjects. To keep the specimen in take for long time they are packed with preservatives.

Diorama

It is an arrangement through which one can visualize the image of a place or a person or anything in a 3 – D way.

Puppets

A puppet is an inanimate object or representative figure animated or manipulated by a puppeteer. It is usually but no means always a depiction of a human character and is used in puppetry, a play or a presentation that is very ancient form of theatre.

Objects

3 – D model is a representation of a physical object.

Mock – Up

Full scale working model of something built for study or testing or display.

Activity Aids

Field trips

Understanding of facts and materials in the real life situation is possible by arranging field trips. It bridges the gap between the real life situation and class room teaching.

The things to be seen ranges widely according to the subjects matter and the need of the students.

Experimentation

It is also used to test the existing theories or new hypothesis in order to support them or disprove them.

Demonstration

Learning by doing through demonstration gains active participation of learner in the extension teaching – learning process. Demonstrations arouse the interest and improve the learning by doing. Seeing is believing. It is the best way to show how a thing works, the end results of the method adopted.

Dramatization

Dramatization helps to provide speak clearly, fluently and expressively. This stimulates the imagination of the pupils. The teacher may tell the class a story / situation assigns the role and asks each of the groups to have separate discussion on how to enact the short play or script. He gives them time to work out the dialogue with or without the help of their teacher. The students discuss and note down movements and facial expression. The students rehear seal thin dramatization it provides fun and excitement in the classroom.

UNIT – IX

EVALUATION IN COMPUTER SCIENCE

The present day education system aims at developing not only physical and mental abilities but also other factors of personality like developing good attitude, interest, critical thinking and social skills. But, the present examination system testing students' memory power and the student's abilities are based on the marks obtained in examination.

Only examination dominates present day education system. It influences schools, teachers, and students. Parents are particular that their children get high marks in final examinations. Therefore, the subjects to taught and learnt are limited by exams. The method of teaching also is based on examination. The teacher who enables more number of students to pass exam, is considered as best teacher.

Tutorials, Guide books, have become important aspects of education system. The knowledge gained over one complete year is tested in 2 to 3 hours to decide the fate of students. There are several defects of examination system, still we can not totally avoid examination system. It has become a necessary evil.

Uses of Test and Examinations

Now-a-days, to assess the development of students in various domains, different types of tests (and tools) are used of which, the achievement test is used to as certain how far they have learnt the subject according to the objectives set forth. In order to find the difficulties of students, and the level and area of difficulties, diagnostic tests are used.

In general, tests and examinations serve the following purposes and hence has become a necessary evil.

1. To know the progress of students in respective areas/subjects.
2. To assess the effectiveness of teaching methods and the teaching aids used and to make necessary modifications, if required.
3. To understand the deficiencies of students and to remedy the problems/deficiencies.
4. Tests are useful for grouping students on the basis of marks obtained, for engaging them in group activities.
5. Exams are useful for planning the school activities/teaching for specific periods-quarterly, half-yearly etc.
6. Employers and Industries use the results and marks for selecting candidates.
7. For promoting students to higher classes.
8. To evaluate the impact of curriculum and education system.

Terms the degree to which a pupil possesses a particular characteristic. The number could be marks or points.

Evaluation

Evaluation is a concept which is more comprehensive than measurement. Marks will not reveal in what position the student stands in the class. 60 marks in history may be first where as it may be the last mark in maths exam. The marks need interpretation with the help of other information.

So, Evaluation = Measurement + value judgments.

Complete and comprehensive evaluation will be useful for providing guidance and counselling also.

Education is a process of bringing about purposeful changes in pupil's behaviour. The direction of this change is determined by the goals or objectives of teaching. Evaluation requires a clear concept of goals the educator wishes to reach by means of instruction. This involves the ways and means of measuring the extent to which these goals are realized. It implies some kind of measurement. But evaluation places a value on it. Evaluation is a continuous process and constantly guides the teacher and the student to attain the goals of instruction.

Objective based teaching and Evaluation

Evaluation attempts to measure a wide range of objectives. It is connected with total personality development. Evaluation is integrated with the whole task of education and its purpose is to improve instruction and not merely to measure its achievement. The relationship between evaluation and the instructional process can be illustrated as follows:

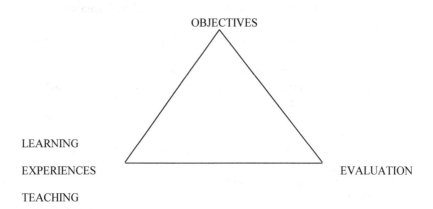

OBJECTIVES

LEARNING

EXPERIENCES   EVALUATION

TEACHING

Teaching process consists of formulating the objectives for the unit, organizing the learning experiences with a view to achieving the specified objectives and finally devising evaluation procedures to check whether the objectives have been achieved.

Evaluation helps the teacher to modify the objectives sometimes or to alter the teaching procedures if necessary or even to check the effectiveness of the tools of assessment.

Concept of Evaluation

Examination

Tests are conducted at small intervals – daily test, weekly test, monthly test. Examination is conducted over a long period on several units taught up to the period of examination quarterly exam half-yearly exam, annual exam etc.

These are useful in assessing how far the teaching organized for achieving the objectives already fixed. Examination is an end event and objective based teaching is the means. The effectiveness of means is assessed through end results. In short, exams are targets to be achieved by teachers and students. It reveals the students' achievement. It enables them to revise these studies. Exam is a tool for evaluation and exam itself is not evaluation.

Measurement

Measurement is an important feature in our daily life. Different types of measurements are made in all aspects of human activity. It is also indispensable in the domain of education.

Measurement is a matter of determining "how much or how little, how great or how small, how much more than or how much less than". In educational process, we often try to find how much the students have gained as a result of instruction. For making that measurement, we need a tool i.e. an achievement test.

In practice our examination system has been criticized and condemned universally by all educationists and educational commissions. Is there any alternative to the system of examination? There seems to be none in the present situation. However, the field of examination has undergone quite a lot of changes and a new concept 'evaluation' has emerged in the place of measurement.

In brief, measurement is making a statement, stating a fact; but evaluation is passing a verdict, making a judgement. The various evaluation tools to be used to determine the student's achievement and the ideal way of preparing a question paper are discussed in this unit.

Measurement and Evaluation

Often, measurement of length, breadth, height, weight is taken in life. As there are infallible measuring devices, the possibility of errors in measuring the physical phenomena is very little. But in educational process, as measurement involves the mental processes of the individual which are not tangible; it is not precise. In education, measurement involves the assignment of a number to express in quantitative measures. We have studied in detail the objectives of teaching computer science in unit 2.

The objectives constitute the core for both teaching and testing and evaluation.

Evaluation is comprehensive including cognitive, affective and psychomotor domains.

Tools and Techniques in Evaluation

In order to evaluate the total personality of students, we need many psychological tools in addition to achievement assessment through examination. Let us examine in brief some of the major tools used for evaluation of students over and above mark assigning exams.

Observation related tools

Though observation itself is not a tool but it is an effective process for evaluation using tools to record observed facts.

Observation is the process of keenly and directly watching student or a phenomenon or the class to identify the characteristics behaviour.

Though the technique itself may not be objective in nature but when used along with other observation tools, it becomes a better technique.

Some of the tools which would be useful are:

    i.   Check list
    ii.   Rating Scale
   iii.   Anecdotal record
   iv.   Cumulative record
    v.   Test and examination
      a. Written test
      b. Oral test or viva voce
      c. Practical / Activity based test / skill test

Check list

This is useful to note down the important changes expected from students, as otherwise the items may not be remembered. This list will be varying from subject to subject. This list should be comprehensive to note down important achievement events.

A check list to note down the progress of students in computer science is given below:

Check list on Computer Science

Name of School _____   Year_____

Teacher's Name_____   Class_____

Students Name_____

Traits (tick relevant box)

a) Skill in using computers

    i.   Works fast but wrongly   ☐

    ii. Works slowly but correctly   ☐

    iii. Works fast and correctly   ☐

b) Skill of drawing

    i.   Understands steps and draws flow charts   ☐

    ii. Skill in drawing logic gate diagram   ☐

    iii. Able to find combination of logic gate diagrams   ☐

c) Skill in problem solving

    i.   Not knowing the steps of problem solving method   ☐

    ii. Not solving systematically but solves by trial and error   ☐

    iii. Not checking the solution   ☐

d) Skill of using software

    i.   Uses fast, without errors/mistakes   ☐

    ii. Does slowly   ☐

    iii. Struggling without understanding   ☐

e) Preparing Truth Tables

    i.   Prepares fast without mistakes   ☐

    ii. Does slowly, hesitating at every stages   ☐

    iii. Struggles without knowing how to proceed   ☐

Rating Scale

Rating scales with five point ratings are better tool than check list, for evaluating special and specific features, skills, qualities, etc.

For each and every characteristic or trait, the rating should be marked either by circling or ticking.

Sl.	Trait	Points		(Totals)		
1	Skill of using computer	1	2	3	4	5
2	Drawing diagrams (skill)	1	2	3	4	5
3	Problem solving skill	1	2	3	4	5
4	Skill of using software	1	2	3	4	5

Note the highest is 5. If we total al ratings for the individual student we will get a total evaluation of the boy in those skills.

Based on the total points we can grade the students, Excellent – A, Good – B, Satisfactory – C, Fair – D, Poor – E.

The rating scale could also be studied by students and understand in which area or skill they are weak and in which they are strong. They can take efforts to improve in weak areas.

Anecdotal record

This is a record of real incidents relating to the student brought to the notice of the teacher. While recording the anecdotes or incidents teacher should avoid including their own subjective recorded. But teacher can have his/her own view in a separate note.

Through this record of natural way of identifying the qualities of students, we can understand not only about their skills but also about their aims, objectives, habits, attitudes, likes and dislikes emotional balances etc. If properly recorded, it will speak about the total personality of the student.

Cumulative Record

For every student, all aspects of evaluation – physical, intellectual, interest, attitude educational, social and emotional aspects of evaluation – made are consolidated year wise in a record note book with specific space provided for each aspect. It is termed as cumulative record. It gives the total profile of the student and could be used for guidance and progress.

Tests and examinations

The education system mainly consists of teaching, learning and evaluation. Evaluation indicates not only students achievement but also it indirectly imply teacher ability to teach.

Test and evaluation and teaching are interdependent activities. There is a maxim which states. Teach-test-teach. Testing is a continuous process and the concept of conducting major examination only is not scientific.

Especially in computer science, every topic requires certain previous knowledge and it builds upon one concept over the other logically and step by step. So, if the basics are not understood, higher concepts can not be understood.

In old system of evaluation, only final result was considered. The steps in between were not given any weight age. In modern evaluation, even if the end result is wrong, marks are given for correct steps.

In old system mostly big problems or essay questions only were given. In modern evaluation all new types of questions are also asked, so that the total syllabus could be covered. Further in modern evaluation, apart from testing, students power of understanding, application abilities, skill are all tested and evaluated.

Different kinds of tests based on purpose

- Ability tests
- Inventory tests
- Practice test
- Achievement test
- Diagnostic test
- Prediction test

Ability tests

If a student wants to pursue computer science education, the ability or skill test will ascertain whether he/she has required skill for studying the course. This could be useful for guidance to take up ability based courses/jobs. This could also be useful to identify the able student from students lacking the abilities.

But for success in any field, apart from ability, students must also work hard and develop good attitudes.

Inventory test

This enables to analyse the previous knowledge and their deficiencies of students who takes up computer science course. It may take long time to identify the lack of pre-requisite knowledge.

Instead, an inventory test will reveal the students deficiencies in advance and take necessary follow up during the course.

Practice Test

This is provided to test how far a student has practiced in specific skills taught. In this, students should complete the test within the time prescribed. In computer science, we need more of this kind as practice makes perfect.

Achievement Test

This is the major test regularly conducted in schools to know the achievement of students in the lessons taught. This is conducted as weekly or monthly tests (formative evaluation) and annual examination (summative evaluation).

There are several modern techniques developed in preparing, conducting and evaluating achievement tests. We will discuss it in detail after discussing different kinds of tests.

Diagnostic Test

This test is specifically conducted to understand the difficulties of students in the topic conducted. This is required to remove the difficulties and misunderstandings of students. Teacher should not hesitate if necessary even to change or modify their methods.

Diagnostic measures and Remedial Education

Remedial education is meant for the students who are in need of it in order to overcome their learning difficulties. The students termed slow learners, backward or who by one or the other reasons show poor performance in learning are provided such education. For instance there is a student who repeatedly shows poor performance in the achievement tests, is unable to answer questions put to him in the class, neglects his home task, demonstrates inability to perform certain experiments or drawing appropriate inferences from the collected data, etc.

The observation of such behaviour of the student in the teaching and learning of computer science may be labelled as a slow or retarded learner. In such a case the teacher is bound to go deep in diagnosing the extent, nature and cause of his weaknesses and difficulties. Such diagnosis may help for bringing about some remedial measures for correcting the weakness and difficulties of the student. Remedial education or teaching in this way must be preceded by a well-planned and properly carried out diagnosis.

Diagnostic Measures

Diagnosis is necessary before any prognosis or prescription. The real nature of the weakness and difficulty faced by the student must be known beforehand for trying about any remedial measure. This diagnosis must be as intensive as possible. The following measures for instance, may be taken for such a diagnosis:

- Physical and medical check-up of the student.
- Preparation of case history by paying attention to his physical and mental health, environment in the family, neighborhood, school and the society, his social and emotional make up, cumulative record, etc.
- Probing about his interests, attitudes and adjustment in the school.
- Interaction with him, observation of his behaviour, questioning, assignments, project work, etc.
- Diagnostic tests.

Whole the measures listed in the first three categories are helpful in probing into the possible causes of the deficiency, the measures belonging to the last two categories are helpful in the identification of the specific areas of weakness or difficulty like following:

i.   The intensity and gravity of the weakness and difficulty
ii. Whether it is of general or specific nature.
iii. Whether the remedial measures can be dealt with in a group or class as a whole or should be tackled on the individual level.

Diagnostic Test and Achievement Test

Achievement tests are conducted to test the achievement of the students after going through a piece of instruction or gaining the desired experiences in a course of formal or informal instruction. When a teacher teaches his lesson or a unit of the curriculum, he may resort to such achievement tests. Such tests may be held after a fixed period in the form of weekly, monthly, quarterly, half year or yearly tests. These may serve the various purposes like selection, certification, promotion etc. and help in the task of taking decision on the quality of learning and effectiveness of the process of instruction.

The diagnostic tests, on the other hand, are purely meant for diagnosing the weakness, deficiency and difficulties of the students related to the specific areas and aspects of the formal and informal learning of a subject. These are constructed not to assess the level of achievements or gains in the learning experiences of the pupils but

151

to reveal the weaknesses and learning difficulties. Hence diagnostic testing should never be confused with achievement testing.

Characteristics of Diagnostic Test

In contrast to achievement test it is found to possess the following characteristics. It aims at analyzing or probing but not at assessing or measuring.

a) It is not a speed test. It allows the pupils to complete all items they are able to do or perform.
b) It is quite intensive and thorough as well as deep and penetrating in probing into the weaknesses and difficulties.

Comparison of diagnostic and achievement

S.No.	Diagnostic Test	Achievement Test
1.	**Objective** To identify the students specific **difficulties** in knowledge or developing skills in the subject.	To measure the **achievement** of the students in the total knowledge and skills of the subject taught.
2.	**Quantity of matter tested** **Small**, specific portion	**Whatever taught** during the period of testing.
3.	**Sampling** Whichever portion is selected, it should be completely covered. Questions could be in **different forms** on same matter.	It is to cover the **entire lessons** taught and hence sampled question could only be asked.
4.	**Difficulty level of questions** The main aim is to find out the difficulties of students and hence questions will be simple.	Easy, medium, difficult questions will be asked to differentiate, three different levels of students.
5.	**Time / Duration** Duration **need not be fixed**. They should try to them at their own pace.	Time duration is **fixed**.
6.	**Analysis of test results** Each students' ability to work every question of the test are analysed to find the difficulty areas for each student.	A casual analysis of the performance is made. If all students are making mistakes in specific problems that will be considered.

7.	**Mark attainment** It is **not at all a major consideration** if they have taken less, the reasons and areas of difficulties will be analysed.	Total mark obtained in the test in **important.** Students' achievements are based on total marks.

Diagnostic tests have to be prepared for every lesson for findings the difficulties of students. Then according to the needs of the students remedial measures have to be taken. This is an important aspect which school education system is mostly ignoring because of growing interest in private tuitions. If these aspects of diagnostic and remedial measures are taken up in schools, the quality of school education will be improved.

Remedial Measures

Remedial measures or education involving corrective steps are to be undertaken for removing weaknesses, deficiencies and difficulties of the learner in order to obtain desired mastery level or optimum educational growth in terms of the specified learning objectives. Its aim is not confined to remove the learning difficulties and overcoming the deficiencies but to provide such congenial environment, facilities and opportunities to the learners as to develop their potentialities to the maximum.

What is Remedial Teaching?

Some of the remedial teaching techniques are briefly discussed here.

1. **Class Teaching**: In this system or schedule of remedial teaching, the usual composition and structure of the class is not disturbed. The teacher here teaches a particular lesson/unit, emphasizes a point again and again, repeats the experiments or uses some specific teaching aid in order to remove the difficulties and deficiencies of the learners in terms of the acquisition of the desired learning experiences. The class as a whole is benefited through such type of remedial teaching. It proves particularly useful in the removal of the weaknesses and learning difficulties of the general nature.

2. **Group Tutorial Teaching**: Here the students of the class are divided into some homogeneous groups called tutorial groups on the basis of their common learning difficulties and identical weaknesses or deficiencies in the acquisition of the learning experiences. These groups are then taught separately by the same teacher of different teachers. The tutor in charge of a tutorial group tries to solve the difficulties of the learners. The group tutorial teaching proves advantageous over the class teaching in many aspects. Here the students who have common problems and difficulties in their learning are helped in overcoming their difficulties and deficiencies. It makes the task of teaching-learning goal oriented. Moreover, the number of students in group tutorial teaching is comparatively

reduced. It results in making the task of teaching more convenient, and effective for providing better coaching and practice in terms of the needed remedial education.

3. **Individual Tutorial Teaching**: In this schedule every learner, who feels learning difficultly is attended individually. It is one to one coaching, help and guidance that is rendered by the teacher to the learner as and when needed by him in order to actualize his potentialities to the maximum. Here the student may progress according to his own pace, abilities and capacities and get adequate help, individual attention and reinforcement.

4. **Supervised Tutorial Teaching**: In this schedule of remedial teaching the responsibility of overcoming the learning difficulties in some learning areas is handed over to the learners themselves. They have to work on their own for removing their difficulties and deficiencies. The role of the teacher is confined to observe and supervise the learning activities and provide as much help as necessary to carry on their path of self learning and self correction. The students may opt to work in the group or individually for solving their difficulties and overcoming their learning deficiencies.

5. **Auto-Instructional Teaching**: This type of remedial teaching consists of auto-instructional programmes and activities. Here the learner is provided with basic auto-instructional and self-learning materials like programmed learning, textbooks and packages, auto-learning modules, teaching machines and computer assisted programmed instruction etc. This material helps the pupil to gain sufficient practice and drill work in the areas of his weakness and acquire necessary confidence in overcoming his difficulties.

6. **Informal Teaching**: Informal science education suitably planned and assimilated with the formal science education of the school may go in a big way to act as a source and means of remedial educational to the needy students. The activities connected with such informal education are in the form of excursions or field-trips, collecting material for the science museum, improvising science apparatus, working on useful scientific projects, engaging in the scientific hobbies, establishing in the school campus and participating in the science club activities. These activities suit the diversified interests of the students and provide unique and special opportunities to learn and practice the facts and principles of science. The learning difficulties arise out of the lack of interest, non-availability of direct and first hand learning experiences, deficiencies in the methodology of teaching, psychological needs and problems of the learners and host of other reasons may be easily overcome through the organization of useful non-formal activities of scientific interest in the schools.

Prediction of Prognosis

Prognosis means foretelling the course of the disease; after observing the students performance over a period, the teacher will be able to predict, specific students may be having certain difficulties and deficiencies. This he judges by seeing his/her overall behaviour and getting grades in the tests of various kinds.

The prognosis or prediction could be confirmed through other tests, especially diagnostic test, as doctors do in the case of their patients. The diagnostic results help to confirm the prediction / prognosis.

Practical Tests in Computer Science

Computer Science as the latest science requires many skills in solving problems some of them are:

- Observation skill
- Critical thinking skill
- Collection of data
- Analysis of data
- Formulation of Hypothesis
- Using input, output devices and finding the solution
- Tabulating data and explaining them/interpreting them.
- Drawing skill (logic gate, flow chart etc)

Many of these skills are developed through laboratory work. Therefore practical test are essential in computer science.

Uses of Practicals

1. To know whether students are able to integrate the knowledge gained and skills learnt, to acquire practical knowledge in the subject.
2. To test observational skills, skill of using of tools and equipments and critical reviewing of the activities.

While conducting practical all the devices and programs must be set ready and the problem must be given. Marks may be assigned for:

1. Collecting data after doing the experiment / program.
2. Explain how the experiment was done.
3. All aspects of practical.
4. It depends on the practical problem to be assigned.

Techniques of evaluation

Continuous and comprehensive Evaluation

Evaluation is done in many ways. It is common practice that students' performance is evaluated at the end of each term viz., quarterly, half yearly and annually. Some teachers are in the habit of evaluating students quite frequently.

In some schools students are evaluated throughout the year for their performance in co-curricular activities besides their achievement in the subjects. This is called continuous comprehensive evaluation.

In these situations, every test serves a definite purpose. Tests and examinations conducted by the teachers can be classified as Criterion referenced and Norm referenced from the point of view of interpreting the results. Tests are also classified as formative and summative from the view point of periodicity.

Norm-referenced tests and Criterion-referenced tests

Criterion based test

Criterion-based tests (CRT) emphasize that teacher should interpret the test results not in comparison to the performance of the group but in relation to a specific performance criterion. A properly constructed CRT reflects all instructional objectives and it helps the teacher to know whether his students have achieved, all of them as a result of his teaching. It helps the teacher to know the weaknesses of individual student in the achievement of the stipulated objectives and there by affords an opportunity for him to modify his technique of teaching. CRT aims at mastery in learning by adopting efficient learning strategies.

Norm based Test

Testing is done to measure student performance after teaching, with a view to finding out whether learning has taken place. Based on their performance students are given numerical marks or grades. But the marks or grades are meaningless unless they are interpreted. So the common practice is to compare the performance of a student with a certain norm i.e. local, regional or national.

A student's performance is compared with others performance to fix his relative position in the group by stating the rank or percentile rank. In a standardized test, the group is carefully selected and well defined representing different age levels on a national, regional or state level. Norm-based tests assume that individual differences in learning exist, as all students do not possess the same intellectual abilities.

Formative and Summative Tests

In teaching situations, a teacher would like to know the impact of his teaching as soon as he completed teaching a unit, by means of a test. This helps him to know the efficiency of his teaching. The results also provide a feedback to the students for monitoring his progress in learning, his weakness and to take remedial measures to correct his learning. Such a kind of test which is frequently conducted by the teacher is called formative test. On the other hand when evaluation is done at the end of the course of instruction, it is called summative test.

Formative tests are meaningful when the results of the tests are discussed with the students and the weaknesses of the students are identified and remedial means suggested. In formative testing, the emphasis is on diagnostic questions.

Summative tests which are given at the end of the course are to assess the overall performance of students and not intended to monitor the progress of students. This is useful to assign course grade and certification.

Criteria of Good Test

Validity

A test should measure what it intends to measure and not what we do not want to measure. For e.g., A test on computer science meant for measuring the acquisition of scientific knowledge should only measure scientific knowledge and not linguistic ability of the student.

It the validity is based on experience, it is empirical validity. If it based on rational conclusion it is rational validity. It could also be predictive validity or concurrent / status validity.

Reliability

A test is reliable when it functions consistently. It must function similarly with similar groups. It should rate the same candidates at the same score even if it is examined by the same or different at the same or different times. The difference in score should be negligible.

Objectivity

It should yield the same or nearly the same score, irrespective of the person who scores it. The scorer's personal judgment, likes and dislikes should not influence the scoring.

Practicability

Students should finish the test in the time allotted for it. It should neither be too long nor too short. It should keep the students busy all the time, from disciplinary and administrative point of view. Some provision should be made for individual differences and some questions may be set for brighter students. It should be manageable with in the funds provided.

Others

Scorability

It should be constructed in such a way that the boredom caused by the routine of scoring is cut down to the minimum. It should allow the use of key in marking so that the test sheet is checked more or less automatically and without subjectivity. It saves a great deal of time and simplifies the work of the teachers with the help of scoring key.

Clarity

The directions given should be brief and definite so that pupils are not handicapped with wrong performance due to misunderstanding of directions. The languages of the questions should be simple, understandable, definite and unambiguous.

Comprehensive

It should cover the whole syllabus. Due importance should be given to each topic while setting the paper, care should be taken that minimum choice is given.

Graded

It should be according to the age and intelligence of the students.

Different Types of Tests –Construction and Organization

Types

Based on length of answer, duration provided for writing, mode of answering, tests can be classified into different types. The first broad categories are teacher made tests which may be in oral or written form.

In order to find the achievement of students, different types of tools are employed. Any test that measures the attainments of a student after a period of learning is called an achievement test. The International Dictionary of Education defines an achievement test as a test designed to measure the effects of specific teaching or training in an area of curriculum.

Achievement tests can be classified into two categories which are further categorized as follows:

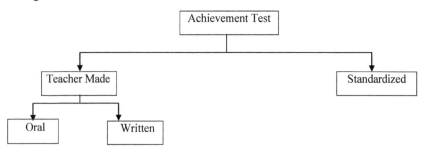

A standardized test is a test consisting of carefully selected test items after having been given to a number of samples under standard conditions. Teachers made test may further be divided into two categories viz. written test and oral test. Written tests can still further be classified as Essay type, Short Answer type and Objective type.

Oral Tests

These are extensively used in lower classes. In higher classes, oral test can be used in science practical examination for assessing the procedures adopted by the students. The viva-voce as used in graduate and post graduate classes is nothing but oral examination.

In classroom teaching, to get immediate feedback from the students on the information provided to them, oral test proves invaluable. However oral tests have certain limitations like time consumption and the subjectivity involved in analyzing the results of the students.

It is pertinent to remember the importance of mental seems asked 5 to 10 minutes in the beginning of a class. This is very useful to consolidate learning and providing drill and practice.

Written Tests

Essay type demand long answers. The essay type requires the student to recall rather than recognize information. Much time is required to answer this type of question as the student has to organize and express his ideas in writing clearly and concisely. Hence only a few questions can be asked within the limited time.

In as-much-as the test cannot cover the entire syllabus, this test is not valid. Further lot of subjectivity is involved in evaluation of the answer script. Besides assessing the quality of the answer, other extraneous factors like neatness in presentation of ideas and good hand writing play a part. However in computer science teaching questions like the following have to be asked.

E.g.   1. Explain enumerated data type with an example.

2. What are the ten commandments of computer ethics?

While preparing answers to this type of question, students have to prepare the outline, organize the material in a proper way and draw neat sketches wherever necessary. These are desirable habits in learning and hence essay type of tests only controls the student's behaviour in acquiring knowledge.

Short answers type questions

Questions that demand answer in a paragraph or few sentences are asked in this category. Students select the relevant information of facts which explain a particular situation for answering the questions.

E.g. write a note on (Computer) virus.

Define operator overloading.

Objective type tests

An objective test is so named because the system of scoring is objective rather than subjective as in the case of an essay test. The objective type tests require specific answers in one or two words. Sometimes it is argued that objective type tests confine largely to the testing of factual information. But the fact is that this limitation is not inherent in the test itself but a limitation of test-writer.

a. True or False test

True or false type items are simple statements which must be either completely false. The student judges the truth or falsity of the statement and indicates suitably with 'T' for true and 'F for false.

e.g. 1. AND gate is a universal gate

e.g. 2. XOR gate is a fundamental gate

b. Matching type

In the traditional format, the matching exercise consists of two column – one column consists of problems to be answered (premises) and the other column contains the answers (responses). The student is required to make some sort of association between each premise and each response.

Student pairs the corresponding elements and records the answers. This type of test can be used to measure pupil's ability to associate events with persons, terms with definitions, principles with examples and chemical symbols with the names of chemicals.

c. Multiple Choice Items

The multiple choice item consists of two parts.

1. The stem which contains the problem or a statement.
2. Three or four responses out of which only one must be correct.

The respondent is asked to choose the correct response and indicate the number in the specified place. The incorrect responses are called distracters. The stem may be a question form or an incomplete statement.

E.g. in how ways polymorphism is achieved in c++?

a) Two
b) Three
c) Four
d) Five
e) Many

Principles of test construction and Administration of Achievement Test

Objective based Evaluation

Planning and construction of an achievement test has become an art and science. Though it may take more time and hard work in the beginning, in due practice, it could become easier.

Planning

1. The objective must be determined for each lesson by analyzing the instructional material thoroughly. Important and new parts, based on objectives, must be included. Portions which could provide training in habits of scientific study, defining from the source information, formulating principles and skill in methods of doing should find a place in the test. The tests should reveal, whether the objectives of teaching the materials have been achieved.
2. Quality of question must be decided and arranged. Questions should not be asked in hap-hazard fashion. The following aspects must be planned.

Construction of Achievement Test

For evaluating students' achievement, an achievement test has to be prepared based on the criteria discussed. It has to be structured and designed according to a systematic pattern by following the 3 major dimensions.

Weightage to Objectives

The main task is to decide the weightage to be given to the different objective formulated while teaching the unit. It is normally easy to test the cognitive area by means of a written test. Under the psychomotor domain also it may be possible to test only one objective under manipulative skill and that too by asking the student to draw neat sketches.

Out of the total marks for which the question paper is set, what is the weightage given to various objectives must be decided.

Weightage to content

Having decided the number of topics to be tested, the teacher has to distribute the total marks to every topic, giving due weightage to the topics based on its importance and number of pages.

Weightage to different forms of questions

Although different forms of tests questions are available, every type has got advantages and limitations. Hence, in testing the learning outcomes, essay type, short-answer type and objective type questions may be judiciously used. Out of the total marks set for the question paper, how much weightage to be given for different types of questions should be decided.

Weightage to Difficulty level

If in a question paper 70% students could answer a question, it is an easy question. If answered by 70 to 30 percent, it is average question. If answered by 30% it is difficult question. There must be more average questions in an ideal test.

Blueprint for the question paper

The blue print is a major three dimensional chart showing the weightages given for objectives, content and form of questions. Blueprint is a document which gives a complete functional picture of the test. To prepare a blueprint the weightages in terms of marks to objectives content areas and forms of questions are first put down in the total column and the cells are then subsequently filled to indicate the position of questions. The total of the marks is indicated in the cells. Both column – wise and row – wise total must tally with the final total.

Preparation of question paper

Once the blue print is prepared, the actual preparation of the test starts. Test items must be prepared based on the particular objective. Some sample items based on the objectives are indicated below. Further the question paper setter is expected to prepare the marking scheme for the essay type questions and very short answer questions beside the key for the objective test items. This will help the examiner to be as far as possible objective in his evaluation.

A model design of the question paper is given below.

Design of the question paper

A weightage to objectives

Objectives	Marks	Percentage
Knowledge	12	24
Understanding	16	32
Application	12	24
Skills	10	20
Total	**50**	**100**

(Note : This percentage may vary depending upon the nature of the lessons / units. In some units there may be opportunity for asking more application and skill questions but in some topics, it may not be possible. The unit may be more knowledge oriented one.)

Weightage to content

Content	Marks	Percentage
Introduction	5	10
Binary Numbers	15	30
Other number systems	15	30
Boolean Algebra	15	30
Total	**50**	**100**

Hence also the weightage is based on the objectives to be achieved and importance of the topics in this respect.

Weightage to forms of questions

Type	Marks	Percentage
Objective type	10	20
Short Answer	10	20
Long/Essay type	30	60
Total	**50**	**100**

In fact, this is decided by the question paper pattern as fixed by the Board of studies. The choice,whether internal choice or total choice, all these are also fixed by the Board. Internal Choice is better but still it is difficult to frame questions of same difficulty levels.

Weightage to Difficulty level

Difficulty Level	Marks	Percentage
A.Difficult	12	24
B.Average	16	32
C.Easy	22	44
Total	**50**	**100**

Fixing the difficulty level I itself difficult but still depending upon analysis of steps and sub-marks, the level can be fixed.

Scheme of options

Scheme of option is about choice provided in answering questions. Because of choice, students learn to omit 40% to 50% of lessons and still get good marks, this is against the principle of evaluation. To restrict the bad effect of choice, internal choice system has been evolved. The choice within the same lesson / unit the internal choice is suitable for essay type questions and not others.

Divisions in Question Paper

Part I or A could b multiple choice and other one mark questions like completion type. Part II or B may be short answers and Part III or C may be essay questions.

Sequence of Questions

According to psychological principles the questions must be from simple to difficult ones, but in practice the orders of the lessons or units is maintained so that student could decide from which unit the question is asked.

Blueprint Preparation

Blue print is based on the tentative plan worked out in Design Stage. Blueprint covers all the dimensions in a tabular form.

Scoring key

This consists of value points or outline answers and marking scheme.

This is done at the time of preparation of question paper itself. This will avoid unexpected mistakes in the questions frames. In computer science, some questions may be more complex than expected or not having any practical solution. Such question could be avoided while preparing the scoring key.

Question wise Analysis

All questions must be analysed on the basis of its objectives. This could be compared with Blueprint. The following headings could be used for analysis:

    a) Objective of the question
    b) Specific objective (SIO) of the question
    c) Topic and sub topic of the question
    d) Type of question
    e) Expected difficulty level
    f) Expected required time
    g) Marks allocated

Computer-Aided-Evaluation

All aspects of evaluation from fixing objectives to question wise analysis including design, blueprint, valuation, analysis of performance could be done with the aid of computer by developing proper programmes.

Since the process of formulation of scientific questions involves several complex process like finding item difficultly value, Index of discrimination etc a computer program could convert the drudgery into a pleasant task. Similarly if the questions are fixed response items, the computer evaluation is made very simple by asking students to mark the answer in OMR sheets.

Any repletion of questions in compilation could be easily identified in computer formulation and analysis.

Further all statistical analysis of the marks/grades could be easily done in computer any data required could be retrieved at any time without delay.

Diagnosis and immediate remedial measures could be taken up by monitoring the program of individual students.

Back up programmes or enriched material could be provided to the gifted and differentiated question could be asked for them. Thus computer aided Evaluation will be a boon to schools.

On-line-Examination

We have elaborately discussed the advantages of computer aided of evaluation. Instead of using the services of computers for test construction, administration, evaluation analysis of the data, if we make use of internet through the computers either using LAN, WAN, or web system, the examination becomes on-line-examination.

The advent of computers and the Internet/web system has made the world a global village. Anybody could study and learn from any place, any course conducted at any part of the word at any time through on-line-studies or e-learning and write the examinations on line and get diplomas and degrees.

The internet/web banished the barriers of space and time. You can write the examination on-line for getting your degree through courses organized by universities in London, Australia, America or Singapore, who knows, within decades, you may sit in a satellite and write the examination on-line!.

COMPUTER TECHNOLOGY

Computers are growing in popularity very rapidly. Almost everything one can think of is being run by computers from organizing records to directing traffic. The information Technology (IT) industry is growing at an incredible rate. The impact of computers on our everyday life is monumental. Every time we make a bank deposit, purchase items on a credit card, pay an insurance premium or rent a video movie, innumerable computer operations are involved. Making all these operations happen, behind the scenes, is the work of a vast array of professional: computer programmes, programmer analysts, systems analysts, hardware and software engineers, database managers, etc. As our society becomes more computerized and technologically sophisticated, the need for highly skilled computer professionals increases accordingly.

THE GROWING CAPABILITY OF COMPUTER TECHNOLOGY

The growing shortage of Information Technology professionals translates into real opportunities for job seekers and those interested in entering the IT industry. Challenge, variety and opportunity make IT a rewarding career. Incredible opportunities are available right now in the rewarding, challenging, and exciting profession of Information Technology. There are no limits to where your talents can take you.

Earning Potential

Talented graduates entering the computer field are likely to be well paid. As in the case with any profession, income potential depends on factors such as company size, location, civilian versus governmental employment, one's career track, job title and responsibilities, academic record, and level of skills. Computer careers can be lucrative for young professionals academically distinguished and making outstanding contributions in their field.

Career Options

The computer technology industry on the whole encompasses many fields of professional involvement and advancement. In broad terms, here are some of the career options that graduates can consider.

Computer Science Jobs

Generally speaking, computer scientists are involved in designing computer systems and in researching ways to enhance the practical applications of such designs. Computer scientists address highly theoretical and complex problems associated with making new technology beneficial to all segments of society: academia, the military, civilian businesses, end-user consumers, etc. Included in this group of computer scientists are computer engineers, database administrators, computer support analysts and other technically specialized professionals.

Systems Development Jobs

People working in this field analyze the informational needs within an organization and the ways by which various computer systems should properly relate to each other to enhance the overall operation of the organization. Systems analysts ensure that the functional areas of the organization accounting, marketing, sales, etc-properly communicate with each other. To accomplish this task, systems analysts study and modify the capabilities of the computer hardware and software to meet the challenging demands of an evolving organization.

EDP Auditor Jobs

This is a challenging career option for professionals who have keen interests and skills in computers as well as in accounting and finance. The fundamental goal of EDP (Electronic Data Processing) auditing is to ensure the accuracy, efficiency, and integrity of a company's computer system, which is at the heart of all its business operations. EDP auditors are concerned, in part, with the accuracy of computer input and output as this accuracy relates to the possibility of financial impropriety, security leak or fraud. Along with knowledge of computer systems, programming languages and various applications, EDP auditors need a good understanding of business and financial management. In fact, many EDP auditors hold MBA degrees and / or CA certification.

Consulting Jobs

Graduates who aspire to become computer consultants can follow a number of career paths. Some computer consultants are motivated by strong entrepreneurial instincts. With several years of industry experience, they choose the route of freelance consulting often as stepping-stones for starting their own companies to carve niches in the computer market. Talented young professionals may also consider a career with combined-practice companies, such as prestigious consulting firms, or with major hardware / software suppliers, or with international consulting firms that offer computer consulting as part of turnkey business services. Other rewarding computer careers include sales / marketing support, technical writing and instruction assurance, network engineering, management information systems, and so forth.

Computers in Non-Professions

Even if you are not interested in becoming a computer professional, it is must that you have basic knowledge of computers and the commonly used applications. It is imperative that you become a computer professional-a person who can use computers with ease to perform routine tasks like composing a letter or memo, send and receive, e-mail, surf the Internet, make computer presentations etc, because in today's information age where computers hold the centre stage, computer proficiency is a must for your survival and success.

Academic Preparation

The road to a well-paying, challenging computer career begins with adequate academic preparation.   A four – year degree in computer science, electrical engineering, or information systems is most appropriate. Students who have opted for branches like Mechanical, Civil, etc. also can become computer professionals if they have the right aptitude and skill set. Now almost all branches offer electives in computer related fields.   Even if one does not want to become a computer professional, knowledge of computers and familiarity with the popular software packages is must in today's world. If you are aspiring to become a specialist in areas like CAD/CAM, Workflow automation, then you need to know the software packages in those areas.

Some of the courses that will help in building a good foundation for the IT profession include computer fundamentals, fundamentals of information technology, programming, computer languages, qualitative and quantitative analysis, operating systems, statistical methods, data and file organization, hardware/software interface, application systems, project management, and so on.   In addition to asking the required computer courses, students study other subjects to become well rounded in the business world.   Examples of such subjects are economics, business law, marketing etc.

Learning other languages offer students a competitive edge in job hunting and professional advancement.   Being conversant in French, Spanish, German, or Japanese (as examples) can pay off by opening doors for job-related travel and project work that involves interfacing with people from different culture and language.

Gaining practical work experience through internship and industry training is critically important. The size of the company isn't as important as the variety of duties and responsibilities that go along with the learning experience. Interning with several companies provide students with valuable perspectives on the type of company they will fit in with most comfortably following graduation. So students should make it a point to do industrial training while they are doing their course.

To become well diversified in the computer field, it is important to develop good interpersonal skills. To students contemplating a computer consulting career, the advice is not to wait until your final year to use the resources of career services. Start targeting the companies you'd like to work for and develop the academic profile they expect of a new employee. Also, the students should get a good blend of business skills. It is important to gain diversified work experience-and to specialize in some industry. Whether it is telecommunications, health care, manufacturing or banking, knowing some industry inside out is important for computer consultants.

Some of the skills required for IT professionals (In addition to solid technical knowledge) are summarized below:

- ❖ Should be able to cope up with constant change.

- ❖ Should be able to analyze information, make appropriate decisions and solve problems.

- ❖ Capability to organize and think logically.

- ❖ Should be able to reason abstractly, observe keenly and concentrate intensely.

- ❖ Should be a team player.

- ❖ Must possess proficiency for accurate details.

- ❖ Should understand computer language, equipment and application programs. Some of the possible career options of IT professionals are

- ❖ Computer Systems Manager.

- ❖ Computer Programmer.

- ❖ Document Specialist.

- ❖ System Software Developer.

- ❖ Computer Engineer.

- ❖ Consultant.

- ❖ Artificial Intelligence Specialist.

- ❖ Technical Writer.

- ❖ CAD/CAM Designer.

- ❖ Consultant.

- ❖ Artificial Intelligence Specialist.

- ❖ Technical Writer.

- ❖ CAD/CAM Designer.

- ❖ Quality Control Designer.

- ❖ Ergonomics Program Designer.

- ❖ EDP Auditor.

- ❖ Training Instructor.

- ❖ Database Administrator.
- ❖ ERP Consultant.
- ❖ Statistician.
- ❖ Specification Writer.
- ❖ Customer Engineer.
- ❖ Special Effects (FX) Specialist.
- ❖ System Analyst.
- ❖ MIS Manager.
- ❖ Cryptographer.
- ❖ Telecommunications Specialist.
- ❖ Programmer / Analyst.
- ❖ Project manager.
- ❖ Computer Operator.
- ❖ Information Systems Auditor.
- ❖ Systems Engineer.
- ❖ Teacher.

ROBOTICS

An autonomous robot is a machine able to extract information from its environment and use knowledge about its world to move safely in a meaningful and purposive manner. It can operate on its own without a human directly controlling it. Robots can use different kinds of sensors to view their environment and have actuators to perform actions in that environment. Several techniques from the field of Artificial intelligence, such as reinforcement learning, neural networks and genetic algorithms, can be applied to autonomous robots in order to improve their performance. Common tasks of mobile robots are mapping the environment, localization of the robot's position within that environment and navigating through it. Multiple robots can perform tasks more efficient because they can work in parallel, but one has to be careful not to let the robots interfere in each other's work. The popular behaviour-based robotics approach combines specific behaviors defined in the control system of a robot to perform tasks. Animal behaviour serves as an inspiration source for behaviour based robotics. Pure behaviours consist of stimuli from the robots' sensors that evoke a motor response. Hybrid behaviours also include knowledge in the form of maps or use forms of deliberative reasoning.

A new approach in robotic control is evolutionary robotics that uses evolution as a tool to create increasingly better robot controllers. Genetic algorithms, which are search algorithms based on the principles of natural selection and natural genetics, are applied to evolve the robot's controller program. Different programs are evolved and the best program is selected based on an evaluation of its performance. A question that is still under debate is whether the evaluation of the control program is more efficient when performed with real robots in real-time or in simulation. Recently research has been done on the co-evolution of robot controller and body configuration.

Parts of Robots

Robots are distinguished from each other by the effectors and sensors with which they are equipped. For example, a mobile robot requires legs or wheels, and a tele-operated robot needs a camera. We will assume that a robot has some sort of rigid body, with rigid links that can move about. Links meet each other at joints, which allow motion. Examples of links are the arms or wheels of a robot. Attached to the final links are end effectors, used by the robot to interact with the world. End effectors can be squeeze grippers, screwdrivers, welding guns, paint sprayers, etc.

Effectors

An effector is any device under the control of the robot that affects the environment. Effectors are used in two ways: to change the position of the robot within its environment (locomotion) and to move other objects in the environment (manipulation). To have an impact on the physical world, an effector must be equipped with an actuator that converts software commands into physical motion. The actuators themselves are electric motors or hydraulic or pneumatic cylinders. The correspondence between the actuator motions in a mechanism and the resulting motion in its various parts can be described with kinematics, the study of motion.

Sensors

One of the most important parts of a robot is it's sensors. Sensors provide feedback to the robot about its current condition and allow a robot to reason about the environment. Many different types of sensors have been developed.

a) Proprioception

Like humans, robots have proprioceptive sense that tells them where their joints are. Encoders fitted to the joints provide very accurate data about joint angles. Wheel encoders measure the revolution of the robot's wheels. Based on their measurement, odometry can provide an estimate of the robot's location that is very accurate when expressed relative to the robot's previous location. This localization technique is called dead reckoning. Unfortunately, because of slippage as the robot moves, the position error from wheel motion increases. Other proprioceptive sensors are accelerometers to detect changes in velocity and a magnetic compass or gyroscope system to measure orientation.

b) Force sensing

Force can be regulated to some extent by controlling electric motor current, but accurate control requires a force sensor. Force sensors are usually placed between the manipulator and end effector and can sense forces and torques in different directions.

c) Tactile sensing

Tactile sensing is the robotic version of the human sense of touch. A robot's tactile sensor uses an elastic material and sensing scheme that measures the distortion of the material under contact. By understanding the physics of the deformation process, it is possible to derive algorithms that can compute position information for the objects that the sensor touches. Most tactile sensors can also sense vibration.

d) Sonar

Sonar sensors measure approximate echo distances to nearby obstacles. Sonar provides useful information about objects very close to the robot and is often used for fast emergency collision avoidance. It can also be used to map the robot's environment over a larger area. In the latter case, an array of a dozen or more sonar sensors is fitted around the perimeter of the robot, each pointing in a different direction. This array is called a sonar ring. Sonar works by measuring the time of flight of a sound pulse generated by the sensor that reflects on an object.

e) Vision

To supplement sonar information, a real-time vision or obstacle detection system is often used. As yet, no robot performs complete scene recognition. Instead vision is used selectively and customized to a specific task or problem. For example, structured light sensors can determine the shape of an object by projecting stripes of light on it and stereo cameras provide pairs of images recorded simultaneously for depth calculations.

Systems in Robots

The following are crucial to all mobile robot systems.

a) Mapping

Mapping is the process of constructing a model of the environment based on sensor measurements. There are different approaches to representing and using spatial information. On one side, there are purely grid-based maps, also called geometric or metric maps. In these representations, the robot's environment is defined by a single, global coordinate system in which all mapping and navigation takes place. Typically, the map is a grid with each cell of the grid representing some amount of space in the real world. These approaches work well within bounded environments where the robot has opportunities to realign itself with the global coordinate system using external markers.

b) Localization

Localization is the process of aligning the robot's local coordinate system with the global coordinate system of a map. Localization is particularly important and difficult for map-based approaches that learn their maps, since the accuracy of a metric map depends on the alignment of the robot with its map. Identifying and correcting for slippage and drift is an important issue in map building and localization. Localization can be separated into two sub problems which are position tracking and global localization.

c) Navigation

A navigation system can usually be divided into two parts: a global planner and a reactive collision avoidance module. The global path planner generates minimum-cost paths to the goal(s) using a map. As a result, it provides intermediate goals to the collision avoidance routine that controls the velocity and the exact direction of motion of the robot.

d) Communication

Communication plays a large role in coordinating teams of robots. Communication is not necessary for cooperation but it is often desirable. Range, content, and guarantees for communication are important factors in the design of social behavior. Communication is not free and can be undependable. It can be done explicitly, through direct channels, or indirectly, through the observation of other robot's behaviors or changes in the environment. Various forms of machine learning have been applied to robotic teams, including reinforcement learning and imitation.

e) Reinforcement Learning

Reinforcement learning has been applied to learn new behaviors and to coordinate existing ones. At the moment, it is probably the most popular way of learning in robots. Reinforcement learning systems attempt to learn a behavior by exploring all of the actions in all of the available states (trail-and-error) and rank them in the order of appropriateness. It uses rewards and/or punishments to alter numerical values in a controller. A component capable of evaluating the response is needed to send the necessary reinforcement signal to the control system. This component can be a human watching the robot or a software module programmed to evaluate the robot's actions. The first is called supervised learning, the latter is unsupervised learning. The feedback to the control system provides information about the quality of the behavioural response. It may be as simple as a binary pass/fail or a more complex numeric evaluation. There is no specification as to what the correct response would be, only how well the particular response worked.

f) Social Learning

Social learning is the process of acquiring new (cooperative) behavior patterns by learning from others. Social learning includes learning how to perform a behavior, and when to perform it. The basic forms of social learning can be defined as imitation or mimicry and social facilitation. Imitation involves first observing another agent's actions (either human or robot), then encoding that action in some internal representation and finally reproducing the initial action. Reinforcements can result from a robot's action directly, from observation of another robot's actions, or from observations of the reinforcement another robot receives tensions between individual and group needs can exist. Robots may be strongly self-interested and have no concern for the society's overall well being. Optimization in social robots usually focuses on minimizing interference between robots and maximizing the society's reward.

g) Artificial Neural Networks

In the real world, it is difficult to learn with hand-programmed algorithms. The continuously changing environment and uncertainty caused by these changes requires a flexible learning system. Artificial neural networks provide this. Learning in neural networks occurs through the adjustment of synaptic weights by an error minimization procedure. The advantage of the use of neural networks is the fact that the system does not need to have specific properties for specific problems. The system tries to determine these properties itself. The only thing humans have to do is provide it with training examples and the corresponding action or reinforcement.

h) Behavioural Encoding

To encode the behavioural response that a stimulus should evoke, a functional mapping from the stimulus domain to the motor domain is needed. The robot's motor response can be separated into two orthogonal components, strength and orientation. Strength indicates the magnitude of the response and orientation denotes the direction of action for the response.

i) Knowledge Representations

A controversy exists regarding the role of knowledge in robotic systems. Behavioural roboticists generally view the use of symbolic representational knowledge as an obstacle to efficient and effective robotic control. Others argue that strong forms of representational knowledge are needed to have a robot perform at anything above the level of a lower life form.

j) Genetic Algorithms

Genetic algorithms are search algorithms based on the principles of natural selection and natural genetics, and are particularly suited for optimization problems. Genetic algorithms work with a set of potential solutions to a problem. Every solution is awarded with a fitness rating, which is a measure of the relative success in solving the problem. The best solutions are combined to form new and hopefully better solutions.

Both the controller and the physical characteristics of a robot play a major role in its functionality. The shape, number and arrangement of sensors determine what features of the environment affect the robot and what will not. The physical dynamics of the actuators and the used control program determine the set of possible actions that the robot may use to perform its task. There have been attempts to evolve features of the physical dynamics of a robot while evolving the controller but the results so far have been very thin.

Uses of Robots

Robot is a mechanical or virtual artificial agent. In practice, it is usually an electro mechanical system which by its appearance or movements, conveys a sense that it has intent or agency of its own. The word robot can refer to both physical robots and virtual software agents, but the later are usually referred to as bots. There is no consensus on which machines qualify as robots, but there is general agreement among experts and the public that robots to do some or all of the following move around, operate a mechanical arm, sense and manipulate their environment, and exhibit intelligent behavior, especially behaviour which mimics humans or animals.

Stories of artificial helper and companions and attempts to create them have a long history, but fully autonomous machines only appeared in the 20th Century. The first digitally operated and programmable robot, the animate was installed in 1961 to life hot pieces of metal from a die casting machine and stack. Today commercial and industrial robots are in wide spread use performing jobs more cheaply or with greater accuracy and reliability than humans. They are also employed for jobs which are too dirty, dangerous or dull to be suitable for humans. Robots are widely used in manufacturing assembly and packing, transport, earth and space exploration, surgery, Weaponry, laboratory, research and mass production of consumer and industrial goods.

People have a generally positive perception of the robots they actually encounter. Domestic robots for cleaning and maintenance are increasingly common in and around homes. There is anxiety, however, over the economic impact of automation and the threat of robotic weaponry, anxiety which is not helped by the many villainous, intelligent, acrobatic robots in popular entertainment. Compared with their fictional counter parts, real robots are still benign, dim-witted and clumsy.

Characteristics of a robot

While there is no single correct definition of 'robot', a typical robot will have several or possibly all of the following properties.

- ❖ It is artificially created.
- ❖ It can sense its environment and manipulate or interact with thing in it.
- ❖ It has some ability to make choices based on the environment often using automatic control or a pre programmed sequence.
- ❖ It is programmable.
- ❖ It moves with one or more axes of rotation or translation.
- ❖ It makes dexterous co ordinate movements.
- ❖ It moves without direct human intervention.
- ❖ It appears to have intent or agency.

The last property, the appearance of agency, is important when people are considering whether to call a machine a robot or just a machine.

Classifications of Robots

It is difficult to compare number of robots in different countries, since there are different definitions of what a "robot" is. The International organization for standardization gives a definition of robot in ISO 8373:" an automatically controlled, reprogrammable, multi purpose, manipulator programmable in three or more axes, which may be either fixed in place or mobile for use in industrial automation applications." Thus definition is used by International Federation of Robotics, the Research Network (EURON) and many national standards committees.

The Robotics Institute of America (RIA) uses a broader definition: a robot is a reprogrammable multi-functional manipulator designed to more materials, parts, tools or specialized devices through variable programmed motions for the performance of a variety of tasks." The RIA subdivides robots into four classes: devices that manipulate objects with manual control, automated devices that manipulate objects with predetermined cycles, programmable and servo-controlled robots, with continuous point to point trajectories and robots of this last type which also acquire information from the environment and move intelligently in response.

History of Robots

Many ancient mythologies include artificial people, such as the mechanical servants built by the Greek God Hephaestus. (Vulcan to the Romans), the clay golems of Jewish legend and clay giants of Norse legend and Galatea the mythical statue of Pygmalion that came to life.

In the 4th Century BC, The Greek mathematician Archytas of Tarentum postulated a mechanical steam – operated bird he called "The Pigeon". Hero of Alexandria (10-70AD) created numerous user-configurable automated devices, and described machines powered by air pressure, steam and water. Susong built a clock tower in china in 1088 featuring mechanical figurines that chimed the hours.

Al-Jazari (1136-1206), a muslim inventor during the Artuqid dynasty, designed and constructed a number of automated machines including Kitchen appliances, musical automata powered by water, and the first programmable humanoid robots in 1206. The robots appeared as four musicians on a boat in a lake, entertaining guests at royal drinking parties. His mechanism had a programmable drum machine with pegs (Cams) that bumped into little levers that operated percussion instruments. The drummer could be made to play different rhythms and different drum patterns by moving the pegs to different locations.

Leonardo Da Vinci (1452-1519) sketched plans for a humanoid robot around 1495. Da Vinci's notebooks, rediscovered in the 1685s contain detailed drawings of a mechanical knight now known as Leonard's robot, able to sit up, wave its arms and move its head and jaw. The design was probably based on anatomical research recorded in his vitruvian Man. It is not known whether he attempted to build it.

First Unimate

The first electronic autonomous robots were created by William grey Walter of the Burden Neurological Institute at Bristol, England in 1948 and 1949. They were named Elmer and Elsie. These robots could sense light and contact with external objects and use these stimulate to navigate.

The first truly modern robot, digitally operated and programmable was invented by George Devol in 1954 and was ultimately called the unimate. Devol sold the first unimate to General Motors in 1960 and it was installed in 1961 in a plant in Trenton New Jersey to lift hot pieces of metal from a die casting machine and stack them.

There were more than one million robots in operation world wide in the first half of 2008, with roughly half in Asia, 32% in Europe, 16% in North America. 1% in Australia and 1% in Africa. Industrial and service robots can be placed into roughly two classifications based on the type of job they do. The first category includes tasks which a robot can do with greater productivity, accuracy or endurance than humans, the second category consists of dirty, dangerous or dull jobs which humans find undesirable.

Many factory jobs are now performed by robots. This has led to cheaper mass – produced goods, including automobiles and electronics. Stationary manipulators used in factories have become the largest market for robots.

There are many jobs which humans would rather leave to robots. The job may be boring, such as domestic cleaning or dangerous such as exploring inside a volcano. Other jobs are physically inaccessible, such as exploring another planet, cleaning inside of a long pipe or performing laparoscopic surgery.

Kinds of jobs done by Robots

Domestic Robots

As Prices fall and robots become smarter and more autonomous, robots are increasingly being seen in the home for cleaning and lawn mowing.

Tele Robots

Tele robots are controlled from a distance by a human operator. The robot may be in another room or another country, or may be on a very different scale to the operator.

Military Robots

Tele operated robot air craft, like the predator are increasingly being used by the military. These pilotless drones can search terrain and fire on targets. Hundreds of robots such as in I Robot's Packbot and the Foster-Miller TALON are being used in Iraq and Afghanistan by the U.S. military to defuse roadside bombs or explosive devices.

Soft Robots

Robots with silicone bodies and flexible actuators (air muscles, electro active polymers and ferrofluids) controlled using fuzzy logic and neural networks look and feel different form robots with rigid. Skeletons are capable of different behaviours.

Swarm Robots

Inspired by colonies of insects such as ants and bees, researchers are modeling the behaviour of swarms of thousands of tiny robots which together perform a useful task, such as finding something hidden, cleaning or spying. Each robot is quite simple, but the emergent behaviour of the swarm is more complex. The whole set of robots can be considered as one single distributed system, in the same way an ant colony can be considered a super organism, exhibiting swarm intelligence. The largest swarms so far created include the iRobot Swam and the open-source Micro-Robotic Project swarm, which are being used to research collective behaviours.

Haptic interface robots

Robotics also has application in the design of virtual reality interfaces. Specialized robots are in widespread use in the haptic research community. These robots, called "haptic interfaces" allow touch-enabled user interaction with real and virtual environments. Robotic forces allow simulating the mechanical properties of "Virtual" objects, which users can experience through their sense of touch.

The most prolific author of stories about robots was Isaac Asimov (1920-1992) who placed robots and their interaction with society at the center of many of his works. Asimov carefully considered the problems of the ideal set of instructions robots might be given in order to lower the risk to humans, and arrived at his Three laws of Robatics: A robot may not injure a human being or through in action, allow a human being to come to harm.

A robot must obey orders given to it b human beings, except where such orders would conflict with the first law, and a robot must protect its own existence as long as such protection does not conflict with the First or second Law. These were introduced in his 1942 short story. "Runaround" although foreshadowed in a few earlier stories. Later, Asimov added the Zeroth law: "A robot may not harm humanity or by inaction allow humanity to come to harm" The rest of the laws are modified sequentially to acknowledge this.

"According to the Oxford English Dictionary, the first passage in Asimov"s short story "Liar" (1941) that mentions the first law is the earliest recorded use of the word robotics. Asimov was not initially aware of this, he assumed the word already existed by analogy with mechanics, hydraulics and other similar terms denoting branches of applied knowledge.

Artificial Intelligence (AI)

Artificial intelligence (AI) is the intelligence of machines and the branch of computer science which aims to create it.

Major AI Textbooks define the field as "the study and design of intelligent agents", where an intelligent agent is a system that perceives its environment and takes actions which maximize its chances of success. John MC Carthy who coined the term in 1956 defines it as "the Science and engineering of making intelligent machines".

Among the traits that researches hope machines will exhibit are reasoning, planning, learning communication, perception and the ability to move and manipulate objects.

Al research uses tools and insights form many fields, including computer science, psychology, philosophy, neuroscience, cognitive science, Linguistics, ontology, operations research economics, control theory, probability, optimization and logic. Al research also overlaps with tasks such as robotics, control systems, scheduling datamining, logistics, speech recognition, facial recognition and many others.

Other names for the field have been proposed such as computational intelligence, synthetic intelligence, intelligent systems or computational rationality. These alternative names are sometimes used to set oneself apart form the part of AI dealing with symbols which is often associated with the term "AI" Itself.

History for AI Research

In the middle of the 20th century, a handful of scientists began a new approach to building intelligent machines, based on recent discoveries in neurology, a new mathematical theory of information, an understanding of control and stability called cybernetics, and above all, by the invention of the digital computer, a machine based on the abstract essence of mathematical reasoning.

The platform of Modern AI Research was founded at the conference on the campus of Dartmouth college in the summer of 1956. Those who attended would become the leaders of AI research for many decades, especially John Mc Carthy, Marvin Minsky, Allen Newell and Herbert Sion who founded AI laboratories at MIT, CMU, and standford. They and their students wrote programs that were to most people simply astonishing. Computers were solving world problems in algebra, proving logical theorems and speaking English. By the middle 60s their research was heavily funded by the U.S. Department of Defence and they were optimistic about the future of the new world.

In the 90s and early 21st Century, AI achieved its greatest success, some what behind the scenes. Artificial intelligence was adopted throughout the technology industry providing the heavy lifting for logistics, data mining, medical diagnosis and many other areas. The success was due to several factors-the incredible power of computers today, a greater emphasis on solving specific sub problems, the creations of new ties between AI and other fields working on similar problems and above all a new commitment by researchers to solid mathematical methods and rigorous scientific standards.

General Intelligence

Most researchers hope that their work will eventually be incorporated into a machine with general intelligence known as strong AI, combining all the skills above and exceeding human abilities, at most or all of them. A few believe that authropomorphic features like artificial consiousness or an artificial brain may be required for such a project.

Many of the problems above are considered AI complete. To solve one problem one must solve them all. For example, even a straight forward, specific task like machine translation requires that the machine follow the author's argument (reason), know what it's talking about (Knowledge) and faithfully reproduce the authors intention (social intelligence) Machine translation there fore is believed to be AI Complete, it may require strong AI to be does as well as humans can do it.

Approaches to AI

Artificial intelligence is a young science and there is still no established unifying theory. The field is fragmented and research communities have grown around different approaches.

Cybernetics and brain simulation

The human brain provides inspiration for artificial intelligence researches, however there is no consensus on how closely, it should be simulated.

In the 40s and 50s a number of researchers explored the connection between neurology, information theory and cybernetics. Some of them built machines that used electronic networks to exhibit rudimentary intelligence, such as W. Grey Walter's turtles and the John Hopkins Beast. Many of these researches gathered for meetings of the telelogical society at Princeton and England.

Cognitive simulation

Economist Herbert simon and Allen Newell Studied human problem solving skills and attempted to formalize them, and their work laid the foundations of the field of artificial intelligence, as well as cognitive science, operations research and management science. Their research team performed psychological experiments to demonstrate the similarities between human problem solving and the programs they were developing.

When Computers with large memories became available around 1970, researchers from all three traditions began to build knowledge into AI applications. This knowledge revolution led to the development and deployment of expert systems, the first truly successful form of A1 software. The knowledge revolution was also driven by the realization that truly enormous amounts of knowledge would be required by many simple AI Applications.

In the 1990s AI researches developed sophisticated mathematical tools to solve specific sub problems. These tools are truly scientific, in the sense that their results are both measurable and verifiable and they have been responsible for many of AI recent successes. The shared Mathematical language has also permitted a high level of collaboration with more established fields like mathematics, economics or operations research.

The "Intelligent agent" Paradigm became widely accepted during the 1990s. An Intelligent agent is a system that perceives its environment and takes actions which maximizes its chances of success. The simplest intelligent agents are programs that solve specific problems. The most complicated intelligent agents are rational, thinking human beings. The paradigm gives researchers license to study isolated problems and find solutions that are both verifiable and useful, without agreeing on one single approach. An agent that solves a specific problem can use any approach that works-some agents are symbolic and logical, some are sub-symbolic neural networks and others may use new approaches. The paradigm also gives researches a common language to communicate with other fields such as decision theory and economics that also use concepts of abstract agents.

Many problems in AI can be solved in theory by intelligently searching through many possible solutions.

Knowledge representation and knowledge engineering are central to AI research. Many of the problems machines are expected to solve will require extensive knowledge about the world. Among the things that AI needs to represent are objects, properties, categories and relations between objects, situations, events, states of time, causes and effects, knowledge about knowledge and any other less well researched domains. A Complete representation of what exists is the commonsense reasoning and the areas of problems largely unsolved needs artificial intelligence.

ICT INTELLIGENCE

ICT Intelligence has been defined as ways including logic, abstract thought, understanding, self-awareness, communication, and learning, retaining, planning, and problem solving towards ICT.

COMPUTERS IN OFFICE AUTOMATION

Introduction

Since the dawn of the 1990's genuine efficiencies in the office have occurred because there are better procedures to accompany the machines. Where the computer once simply replicated the previous manual tasks, it now automates more fully. The processes and the procedures have improved.

In this area we will see the two fundamental business computing systems-Office Automation and Management Information systems.

Office Automation

Office automation is defined as using computer and communications technology to help people better use and manage information. Office automation technology includes all types of computers, telephones, electronic mail, and office machines that use microprocessors or other high-technology components.

People who use office automation are often called knowledge workers-senior executives, managers, supervisors, analysts, engineers, and other white-collar office workers. In most offices, information (Often in paper form) is the end product and is essential for conducting the company's business. Office automation systems keep track of the information originating in various operations throughout the company, such as order processing, accounting, inventory, and manufacturing. Office automation provides knowledge workers with information-producing systems to collect, analyze, plan, and control information about the many facets of the business, using text, voice, graphics and video display technology.

People

Although it takes people to complete work, it is the way people work that accounts for productivity. In recent years, the trend has been towards people working together to accomplish more. This is called work-group computing, which means a number of knowledge workers, each with different tasks, jobs or duties, work together towards a common goal. In large companies, there may be dozens or hundreds of workgroups. In smaller companies, everyone is part of the workgroup.

Ergonomics

Business learnt that office could not be automated in the same way the factory was automated, and the field of ergonomic began to emerge. Office tasks involve a great deal of thinking and decision-making. As a result office systems must be flexible and versatile. Moreover, they must be designed so any knowledge worker, regardless of background can easily use them. This is called ergonomics, the study of how to create safety, comfort and ease of use for people who use machines. It is not a new field of study; in fact it has existed for over 100 years.

With the advent of computers, ergonomics engineers became particularly interested in office automation systems, furniture and environments for the knowledge worker. Intensive studies determined the best designs for keyboards, set eye fatigue levels for monitors and specified desk and seating designs that alleviate physical stress. Office furniture companies soon introduced ergonomically designed chairs and equipment. Ergonomics has played a significant role in helping people use technology more effectively.

Office Automation Technologies

There are five primary technologies used in managing information in office automation:

- ❖ Text or written words.

- ❖ Data, as in numbers or other non-text forms.

- ❖ Graphics, including drawings, charts and photographs.

- ❖ Audio, as in telephone, voice mail, or voice recognition systems.

- ❖ Video, such as captured images, video tapes or teleconferencing.

In the past these forms of information was created using different technologies Text was created using conventional typewriters or more recently, word processing. Data, such as sales reports, was provided by the central computer. Charts and graphs were either hand-drawn or created using 35mm slide photography and videotapes were used for training. Audio was limited to the phone or tape recording. It was not possible to combine these various forms of information.

What made it possible to combine them was the computer. What computer produces is called an electronic document, which is a self-contained work, conveying information that has been created by a knowledge worker and stored in a computer system. An electronic document may be a simple memo that may be printed on paper or transmitted via electronic mail. Or it may be a more complex document, with graphics or even video. Most computer systems can incorporate sound, so that an on screen document can be annotated with comments spoken by the document creator.

Today, the computer integrates these different media and others as well. Data, sound and images can all be entered into a computer, stored and translated into the kind of output we need. It is now common to see knowledge workers in workgroups using a special type of software designed specifically of them and their work. This application software, called groupware, lets networked PCs and workstations share information and electronic documents from both corporate and on-line sources. At the centre of this integration are networking and communications systems.

Office Automation Systems

Office automation uses computer-based systems to provide information to help knowledge workers make decisions that benefit the business. Office automation systems are comprised of many distinct subsystems: text management systems business analysis systems, document management systems and Network and communications systems.

Text Management Systems

A text management system is a computer system designed to work with the written or typewritten word. It includes all kinds of typewriters, word processing systems, PC's with word processing, desktop publishing and text editing systems, and even computerized typesetting equipment. Text management systems are used for tasks like writing memos, notes, letters and other short documents, printing envelopes and labels, preparing pre-printed forms such as invoices, composing complex documents such as proposals and reports, retrieving and editing documents such as contracts, creating display documents like newsletters, etc.

Business Analysis Systems

Managers need solid data from which to extract the information necessary to make good decisions for the business. In the past, these knowledge workers had to rely on their experience and other personal factors to make decisions. A business analysis system provides data that, when used with the proper software, helps its users better understand the business environment and make more effective decisions. Corporate users routinely use spreadsheets for analyzing cost and benefits and for creating budgets.

Other software tools for performing analysis that are commonly used in large companies are decision support systems (DSS), expert systems and executive support systems (ESS). A decision support system helps the knowledge worker to extract information form the various MIS database and reporting systems, analyze it, and then formulate a decision or a strategy for business planning. An expert system is a computer system that can store and retrieve data with special problem solving expertise. An executive support system is an information system that consolidates and summarizes ongoing transactions within the organization. It provides the management with all information it requires at all times from internal as well as external sources.

Document Management Systems

Document management systems aid in filing, tracking and managing documents, whether they are paper, computer based, micrographics, or purely electronic. Office automation demands that the data is immediately accessible and instantaneously retrievable. For that reason, we are slowly moving away from paper and towards document forms that can be stored on the computer.

Network and Communication Management Systems

Today, knowledge workers have many ways to communicate with one another, primarily by voice, fax, and e-mail. They can communicate in real-time, via phone or computer. They can also communicate using computer controlled PBX telephone systems to record a digital message and leave it in the recipient's electronic mail box. These systems are called network and communication management systems. The network and communication management systems include telephone, electronic mail, voice messaging systems, Tele conferencing and fax machines.

BIBLIOGRAPHY

Aggarwal JC., (1995), Essentials of educational technology Learning Innovations.

Byran Pfaffenbegrer, (1997), Discover the Internet, Comdex Computer Publishing, New Delhi.

Chauhan S.S., (1985), Innovation in teaching Learning process, Vikas publishing house, New Delhi.

Harley Hahn, (1996), The Internet-complete reference, Tata McGrow Hill Pub.Co.,Ltd., New Delhi.

Kumar K.L., (2000), Educational Technology, New Age International Pvt. Ltd. New Delhi.

Morris Mano, (1996), Digital Design, Prentice Hall of India Pvt. Ltd. New Delhi.

Pangotra N.N., Fundamentals of Educational Technology, Chandigarh, International publisher.

Rao B., Anand and ravisankar S., (1982), Readings in Educational Technology, Bombay, Himalaya Publishing House, 1982.

Sinha P.K., (1992), Computer Fundamentals, BPB Publications, New delhi.

Sharma R., (1988), Technology of Teaching International publishing House, meerut, India.

http://www.learningbyte.com

http://www.msonline.com

http://www.zeelearn.com